Marko Ivan Rupnik

ACCORDING TO THE SPIRIT

Spiritual theology on the move with Pope Francis' Church

LIBERIA EDITRICE VATICANA

PHOTOGRAPHIC ACKNOWLEDGEMENTS:

© https://creativecommons.org/licenses/by-sa/4.0 fig. 1
© https://commons.wikimedia.org/w/index.php?curid=17456087, Public Domain, fig. 2
© http://www.duomomonreale.it/ figg. 3, 4, 5, 6
© www.Biblelandpicture.com/Alamy stock photo, fig. 7
© www.agefotostock.com, fig. 8
© La Maison du Visiteur, Vezelay, figs 9-10

Published in Australia by

© Copyright 2019 Coventry Press

Coventry Press
33 Scoresby Road
Bayswater Vic. 3153
Australia

Translated into English by Salesians of Don Bosco of the Province of Mary Help of Christians of Australia and The Pacific

ISBN 9780648497738

© Copyright 2017 - Libreria Editrice Vaticana
00120 Città del Vaticano
Tel. 06.698.81032 - Fax 06.698.84716
commerciale.lev@spc.va

All rights reserved. Other than for the purposes and subject to the conditions prescribed under the *Copyright Act*, no part of this publication may be reproduced, stored in a retrieval system, or transmitted in any form or by any means, electronic, mechanical, photocopying, recording or otherwise, without the prior permission of the publisher.

Cataloguing-in-Publication entry is available from the National Library of Australia http:/catalogue.nla.gov.au/.

Printed in Australia

www.coventrypress.com.au

SERIES
THE THEOLOGY OF POPE FRANCIS

- JURGEN WERBICK: *God's Weakness for Humankind.* Pope Francis' view of God

- LUCIO CASULA: *Faces, Gestures and Places.* Pope Francis' Christology

- PETER HÜNERMANN: *Human Beings According to Christ Today.* Pope Francis' Anthropology

- ROBERTO REPOLE: *The Dream of a Gospel-inspired Church.* Pope Francis' Ecclesiology

- CARLOS GALLI: *Christ, Mary, the Church and the Peoples.* Pope Francis' Mariology

- SANTIAGO MADRIGAL TERRAZAS: *'Unity Prevails over Conflict'.* Pope Francis' Ecumenism

- ARISTIDE FUMAGALLI: *Journeying in Love.* Pope Francis' Moral Theology

- JUAN CARLOS SCANNONE: *The Gospel of Mercy in the Spirit of Discernment.* Pope Francis' Social Ethics

- MARINELLA PERRONI: *Kerygma and Prophecy.* Pope Francis' Biblical Hermeneutics

- PIERO CODA: *'The Church is the Gospel'.* At the sources of Pope Francis' theology

- MARKO IVAN RUPNIK: *According to the Spirit.* Spiritual theology on the move with Pope Francis' Church

ABBREVIATIONS

AAS *Acta Apostolicae Sedis*

DS *Dictionnaire de spiritualité, ascétique et mystique, doctrine et histoire*

EG *Evangelii Gaudium*

LF *Lumen Fidei*

LG *Lumen Gentium*

PG *Patrologiae cursus completus, series graeca* (J.-P. Migne)

PL *Patrologiae cursus completus, series latina* (J.-P. Migne)

SC *Sources chrétiennes*

PREFACE TO THE SERIES

From the time of his first appearance in St Peter's Square on the evening of his election, it was more than clear that Francis' pontificate would be adopting a new style. His modest apparel, calling himself the Bishop of Rome, asking the people to pray for him – in the 'deafening silence' of a packed square – and greeting them with a simple '*buonasera*' (good evening) … these were all eloquent signs of the fact that there was a change taking place in the way the Pope related to people, and thus in the 'language' used.

The gestures and words that have followed from that occasion only confirm and strengthen this first impression. Indeed, it could be said that over the ensuing years, the image of the papacy has been decidedly transformed, involving a change that affects homilies, addresses and documents promulgated as well.

As could be predicted, this has generated divergent opinions, especially regarding his teaching. While many have in fact welcomed his magisterium with enthusiasm and deep interest, sensing the fresh wind of the gospel, some others have approached it in a more detached way and, at times, with suspicion. There has been no lack of more absolute views, even going as far as to doubt the existence of a theology in Francis' teaching.

A summary judgement of this kind could come from the very different backgrounds of Francis and his predecessor, Benedict XVI. The latter, we know, has been one of the most outstanding and important theologians of the twentieth century and undoubtedly relied on his personal theological development in his rich papal magisterium. We have not yet fully appreciated, nor will we cease to appreciate, the depth of this magisterium. What Bergoglio has behind him, on the other hand, is his long and deep-rooted experience as a religious and a pastor.

However, this does not mean that his magisterium is without a theology. The fact that he was not mostly, or only, a 'professional' theologian does not mean that his magisterium is not supported by a theology. Were this the case, we could say that, strictly speaking, the majority of his predecessors were without a theology, given that Ratzinger represents the exception rather than the rule.

In any case, the fact that we can discuss the theological significance of Francis' magisterium, as well as the fact that, very often, some of his highly evocative and very immediate expressions have been so abused as to rob them of their profundity – in the journalistic as well as the ecclesial ambit – makes the response of this series, which I have the honour of presenting, a significant one.

By drawing on the competence and rigorous study of theologians of proven worth, coming from diverse contexts, the series has sought to research the theological thinking which supports the Pope's teaching. It explores its roots, its freshness, and its continuity with earlier magisterium.

The result can be found in the eleven volumes which make up this series with its simple and direct title: 'The Theology of Pope Francis'.

They can be read independently of one another, obviously; they have been written by individual authors independently of each other. Nevertheless, the hope is that a reading of the entire series would not only be a valuable aid for grasping the theology upon which Francis' teaching is based, in the various theological fields of knowledge, but also an introduction to the key points of his thinking and teaching overall.

The intention, then, is not one of 'apologetics', and even less so is it to add further voices to the many already speaking about the Pope. The aim is to try to see, and to help others to see, what theological thinking Francis bases himself on and expresses, in such a fresh way in his teaching.

Among the many discoveries the reader could make in reading these volumes, would certainly be that of observing how so much of the beneficial freshness of the Council's teaching flows into Francis' magisterium. This is true both of the theological preparation he has had, and of what has followed from it. Given that it is perhaps still too soon for all this wealth to become common patrimony, peacefully and fully received by everyone, it should be no surprise that the Pope's teaching is sometimes not immediately understood by everyone.

By the same token, a point of no return has been reached in Francis' teaching, one that recent theology and the Council have both taught: that doctrine cannot be something extraneous to so-called pastoral theology and ministry. The truth that the Church is called to watch over is the truth of Christ's gospel, which needs to be communicated to the women and men of every time and place. This is why the task of the ecclesial magisterium must also be one of favouring this communication of the gospel. Hence, theology can never be reduced to a dry, desk-bound exercise, disconnected from the life of the people of God and its mission. This mission is that the women and men of every age encounter the perennial and inexhaustible freshness of Jesus' gospel.

Over these years there have been those who have heard some of Francis' own critical statements regarding theology or theologians, and have concluded that he holds it and them in low esteem. Perhaps a more detailed study of the Pope's teaching, such as offered by this series, could also be helpful for showing that, while we always need to be critical of a theology that loses its vital connection to the living faith of the Church, it is also essential to have a theology which takes up the task of thinking critically about this very faith, and doing so with 'creative fidelity', so that it may continue to be proclaimed.

Francis' teaching is certainly not lacking in a theology of this kind; and a theology of the kind is certainly one much desired by a magisterium such as his, which so wants God's mercy to continue to touch the minds and hearts of the women and men of our time.

Editor-in-chief
ROBERTO REPOLE

CONTENTS

Abbreviations 4
Preface to the Series 5

INTRODUCTION

KEY TO UNDERSTANDING 13

   1. A new mentality which corresponds to a new life 16

   2. A systematic overview requires a systematic mentality 18

   3. The ecclesial institution as an icon of Life 22

   4. The shift toward communion 25

   5. From Constantine's throne to Peter's chair 27

   6. Starting out from the person, with the Trinity as background 31

CHAPTER I

A NOTE ON TERMINOLOGY 37

   1. Terms 37

   2. The sense in which we speak of 'spiritual theology' in this book 43

   3. The method 47

   4. The sources of spiritual theology 49

   5. A spiritual outlook on humanity in all its complexity 52

6. 'Through the eyes of faith'............................. 56

Chapter 2

Human existence cannot be reduced to its nature 61

1. *Escaping from death* 61
2. *If the will does not enter into sonship* 64

Chapter 3

Abraham (Abram): From the individual to the person 67

1. *God calls us to a relational existence*............. 67
2. *Abram still as the individual* 72
3. *God is person, his existence is communal* 76
4. *An existence that includes otherness* 80
5. *God communicates his 'tropos' to human beings* 82
6. *The beginning of the spiritual life is acceptance, welcome* 90
7. *The greatness of the gift depends on the welcome shown* 95
8. *Living our humanity according to the life we have received* 101

Chapter 4

The Spirit enables us to know the gift according to God 105

1. *The individual takes possession of every gift and every grace* 105

2. Faith and religion 111
3. The person emerges from sacrifice according to faith 113
4. In the sacrifice of his son, Abraham discovers fatherhood as love, the way God loves 118
5. Unity is protected by love 122
6. From the personal to the individual self 128

Chapter 5

The beginning of the spiritual life 133

1. Christ's sacrifice 133
2. Born into Easter 138
3. From the individual self to the self lived as communion 142

Chapter 6

Life in Christ 147

1. To the Father, through Christ, in the Holy Spirit 147
2. From life destined to die to life that continues 154
3. Food suited to this birth 161
4. Our evil in the body of Christ 166
5. Sharers in the sacrifice of communion 170

Conclusion

The symbol: Humanity as revelation 177

INTRODUCTION
KEY TO UNDERSTANDING

By picking up on pointers in Pope Francis' magisterium, this text is an attempt at a spiritual theology on the move, along with his Church. It will be a spiritual theology which expresses the renewal of ecclesiastical life as outlined by Pope Francis to support the epic period of transition we find ourselves in.

> We, by Baptism, are immersed in that inexhaustible source of life which is the death of Jesus, the greatest act of love in all of history; and thanks to this love we can live a new life, no longer at the mercy of evil, of sin and of death, but in communion with God and with our brothers and sisters.[1]

> This is what the word 'Christian' means, it means consecrated like Jesus, in the same Spirit in which Jesus was immersed throughout his earthly existence. He is the 'Christ', the Anointed One, the Consecrated One; we, the baptized, are 'Christian', meaning consecrated, anointed.[2]

1 FRANCIS, *General Audience*, Wednesday 8 January 2014
2 FRANCIS, *Homily for the Feast of the Baptism of the Lord*, Sunday 11 January 2015.

To be able to live this new life so our humanity can be a theophany, a place which reveals the Father's love for each human being, we need to be careful to avoid the temptations within the Church which corrupt the Christian.

> The first is that of the Pelagian. It spurs the Church not to be humble, disinterested and blessed. It does so through the appearance of something good. Pelagianism leads us to trust in structures, in organizations, in planning that is perfect because it is abstract. Often it also leads us to assume a controlling, harsh and normative manner. Norms give Pelagianism the security of feeling superior, of having a precise bearing. This is where it finds its strength, not in the lightness of the Spirit's breath. Before the evils or problems of the Church it is useless to seek solutions in conservatism and fundamentalism, in the restoration of obsolete practices and forms that even culturally lack the capacity to be meaningful. Christian doctrine is not a closed system, incapable of raising questions, doubts, inquiries, but is living, is able to unsettle, is able to enliven. It has a face that is supple, a body that moves and develops, flesh that is tender: Christian doctrine is called Jesus Christ.

> The reform of the Church then — and the Church is *semper reformanda* — is foreign to Pelagianism. She is not exhausted in the countless plans to change her structures. It

instead means being implanted and rooted in Christ, allowing herself to be led by the Spirit. Thus everything will be possible with genius and creativity ...

May she be a free Church, open to the challenges of the present, never on the defensive out of fear of losing something. Never on the defensive out of fear of losing something. And, encountering the people along the way, she takes on St Paul's aim: "To the weak I became weak, that I might win the weak. I have become all things to all men, that I might by all means save some" (1 Cor 9:22).

A second temptation to defeat is that of Gnosticism. This leads to trusting in logical and clear reasoning, which nonetheless loses the tenderness of a brother's flesh. The attraction of gnosticism is that of "a purely subjective faith whose only interest is a certain experience or a set of ideas and bits of information which are meant to console and enlighten, but which ultimately keep one imprisoned in his or her own thoughts and feelings" (*Evangelii Gaudium*, n. 94). Gnosticism cannot transcend.

The difference between Christian transcendence and any form of gnostic spiritualism lies in the mystery of the incarnation. Not putting into practice, not leading the Word into reality, means building on sand, staying within pure idea and decaying into intimisms that bear no fruit, that render its dyamism barren.[1]

1. *A new mentality which corresponds to a new life*

There is no doubt that the election of Cardinal Bergoglio to the Chair of Peter represents a decisive step in the Church's renewal along the lines suggested by Vatican Council II. In fact there are incontrovertible signs that a second stage of functional maturity in understanding the Council has opened with him.

The critical juncture that Vatican II was for the Church was such that we have needed some decades for the dust stirred up by media discussion to settle, a discussion where practically every one felt authorized to interpret what the Council wanted.

The cultural wave into which Vatican II and its aftermath fell, certainly influenced its first, immediate interpretation. And perhaps it was actually the cultural trends typical of the '60s and '70s which caused an imbalance in this interpretation, especially in terms of experimentation, audacious implementation, break with the past – all things that now seem to be overly characteristic of that era. We are sure that many of the Council's deepest and most prophetic intuitions are still ahead of us and are just waiting for the right moment to bring about a real renewal of the Church.[2]

---

1 FRANCIS, *Address at the meeting with representatives of the 5th Convention of the Italian Church*, Cathedral of Santa Maria del Fiore, Florence, 10 November 2015.

2 Cf. BENEDICT XVI, *Homily at the Mass for the opening of the*

The complex nature of Vatican II can only be translated into Church reform if we have a systematic overview of it.[3]

The problem, however, is that recovering such a systematic overview can only happen by inducing a way of thinking which flows from the life which is the gift of the Holy Spirit. We delude ourselves if we think that Church reform can happen by pouring renewed content into the old approach to theology, which still today continues to be divided into compartments where each one claims the exclusiveness of his or her subject and method. This is not only incapable of being integrated into a coherent whole but also of being a living and adequate expression of the nature of the Church. It is as if the Council's intuitions were sufficient and self-explanatory without the need to overcome the disconnect between theology and the living sources of the Church's life that make theology itself possible as a systematic overview, a witness to the 'mind' of the Church. 'Systematic overview' does not so much mean creating a new, unified and all-embracing system where everything has its place. Rather is it about abandoning the attempt to create an all-encompassing system and instead being led by the life that God gives his Church, so that a vision of communion may emerge from this very life in the slow and patient weaving together of all its bits and pieces.

Year of Faith, 11 October 2012.
3 Cf. FRANCIS, *Address to members of the International Theological Commission*, Hall of Popes, 6 December 2013.

2. *A systematic overview requires a systematic mentality*

We have appropriated Vatican II with models from a fragmented theology which were unable to really take account of the flow of life that led to the Council and which the Council wanted to communicate. A fragmented ecclesial culture also took up Vatican II's teaching in fragmented ways, instead of letting itself be challenged and questioned by the systematic view that the Council was offering. It made Vatican II into 'doctrine', opening the possibility of only a rational understanding as teaching, or even as an ideological reference point, in other words, detached from life.[4]

Clear demonstration of this is that decades of teaching based on Vatican II in our theological atheneums and seminaries have produced nostalgia in us for the Council of Trent. This historical paradox shows that Vatican II has not been taught in accordance with the systematic vision and flow of life which animated it, and that something artificial has happened in passing it on. The flow of the Spirit, of authentic renewal, has diminished. We are more than ever bound to methodologies, academic approaches, in a growing split between theology and the life of the Church, for which theology has become increasingly and palpably insignificant for its life. It is as if, after the initial transmission, we were unable to pass on our love for the Church, the freshness of life and rich appreciation of the inspiration coming from the memory of the tradition which dwelt in the more significant theologians and bishops who

---

4 Cf. FRANCIS, *Address to Rectors and students of the Pontifical Colleges and Residences in Rome*, 12 May 2014.

prepared for and carried out the conciliar event. Indeed many of them – a Romano Guardini from some decades earlier, a De Lubac, a Daniélou, a Congar, just to name some – have had no heirs, and this means that they too have been studied in a fragmented way, taken out of the flow of life that they had interpreted.

This theology, identified with university methods, taught Vatican II in such a way that it brought about its rejection and the nostalgic desire to return to something which was by now culturally cut off from the new era coming into being. What was lacking in this teaching was any grounding in this new life which was the experience of the Church as a body, one that gave an overall view and hence was the foundation for a more comprehensive understanding. We lived in a kind of cultural backwater, as if we wanted to prolong modernity's appeal to reason and its methodologies, while meanwhile the majority culture was entering into a new era with a different cultural sensitivity. Hence, the interpretations of Vatican II and the attempts to realize it remained fragmented.

The most evident manifestation of such a trend has been liturgical reform. Today, perhaps, it is clearer than it was before that it is not possible to promote reform of the liturgy without revisiting the entire ecclesial, theological, missionary, apostolic and pastoral approach. If theology, which is the Church's effort to express the content of the new life, does something other than nourish itself, find its foundation where life is received, lived and manifested – in the liturgy, that is – and develops its own separate categories which it then projects onto the liturgy, then we no longer have either the theological criteria for understanding the true meaning of liturgy or for being able to connect with it in the right way. No liturgical reform is possible without a mutual reintegration of liturgy, theology, spirituality. It is not possible to foster liturgical reform if theology remains imprisoned by an analytical and instrumental rationality. It is not even possible to understand and treasure the wonderfully competent and constructive work which led to liturgical reform without recovering a symbolic mindset of the kind found in the great theological tradition of the first millennium.

It is likewise impossible not to acknowledge the fragmentation if we pick up any manual of pastoral theology. Thumbing through the pages we discover that theology is the smaller part, while there is much more sociology, study of culture, psychology …

And what is to be said about the formation programs carried out by Church institutions where here too, theology is absent or sprinkled like seasoning, but the real substance of the programs draws on other disciplines? These are precisely the result of a formation setup of the kind that makes us clearly see the inability to overcome fragmentation and educate to a more complex and systematic intellectual capacity. We are quickly satisfied with a presumed understanding which nevertheless does not take long to reveal that it is powerless to hold together thought and life, the Church and its theologizing, tradition and the future. An understanding that does not detach itself from reasoning beholden to nature will never arrive at the true key points for encountering the life of the Spirit and hence the life of the Church, that is, divine life as a communion of persons, resurrection, transfiguration and fulfilment in the *eschaton* ... As a consequence, an intellectual approach based on reasoning of this kind never ends up opening a spiritual outlook on the nature of phenomena like pain, suffering, failure, health, well-being, work, rejection, success ... So what formation are we talking about if such questions are not enlightened by a spiritual outlook which makes it possible to speak at a pastoral and experiential level?

The missionary nature of the Church is also distorted without a systematic, theological and ecclesial overview. Although we have gone out on mission in more recent centuries, sometimes raising to the ground what we have found, the attitude after Vatican II has often been one of relativizing the unique role of the incarnation, death and resurrection of Jesus Christ in order to mediate our relationship with God. Without a theological view capable of reasoning in terms of the Easter events, it is clear that we lose out on the real offer of newness that Christ brought to humanity. A sort of heavy relativism sets in, as if mission and evangelization consisted of finding consensus with non-Christians on the values we need to agree on for a better life. The result is that it becomes difficult for a fragmented theology to think with a true theological perspective, that is, a spiritual one nourished by the life of the Spirit given to us in Christ; such life in the Spirit moves, instead, within dogma so that it might learn to think according to the divine life it has received; it draws on a holistic language such as the language assimilated by the liturgy, learning to think with the cosmos, the wheat, the vine, the olive trees, the waters;

it is missionary because it unlocks the world brought to fulfilment in Christ; it offers an absolute novelty from the perspective of the eschatological fulfilment which enters our world with the gift of the Son.

A theology which holds together systematically is the result of an integrating form of theologizing because it avoids the isolationism dividing the divine from the human, insofar as it works on humanity as a theophany, on the divine-human nature of Christ. Hence we are talking about theology as bearer of a liturgical process where we discover one reality through another, ever deeper one. It does not become a dialectical, exclusive way of thinking that creates rifts and antagonisms between various positions presumed to be in opposition, like the one, for example, between faith and science which we have dwelt on for decades. Therefore every theology is at the same time dogmatic, spiritual, missionary, pastoral, moral, biblical because it deals with seeing how the Word enters into human thought, how the coming of the Word into our flesh is a synergy, a convergence with the Holy Spirit. By welcoming the Spirit we are entering into a personal dimension[5] and then we become transformed from within by Christ,[6] Christ bearers. Hence spiritual theology safeguards the nature of theology.

3. *The ecclesial institution as an icon of Life*

What emerges more clearly is that despite any intuitions of Vatican II we might have wanted to give substance to,

5 Cf. *Lumen Fidei* (*LF*), 21.
6 *Ibid*, 20.

the attempt foundered on the rocks of a Church structured in such a way that it failed to welcome the newness on offer. Even great movements which arose after Vatican II and gave rise to such hope found themselves fading after a few decades and in difficulty because they were more and more framed within an institutional form which was old in comparison with the newness of life they had taken up.

Now, it is precisely the flow of life in the Holy Spirit that emerges across the centuries, and in places where the Church is established, that has also demanded a renewal of mentality. It is not possible to theologize on new life with an old mindset. Many of the new realities which arose after Vatican II have found themselves chewing on a way of theologizing that is not an expression of the life from which they arose, is not an integral part of this life.

What we said at the beginning returns as the central issue in the problem: there is a life that the Spirit gives rise to, there is a people on the move, but then it is as if this life gets snuffed out by suffocating procedures and ways of organizing things. So what is needed is for the very life flow that led to Vatican II to return once more, like a subterranean channel, and this time we need to follow it completely if we want to hear what 'the Spirit is saying to the churches' (Rev 2:7).

We can approach organized and structured forms in two ways: on the one hand we can be afraid to touch them, or on the other, we can tackle them in revolutionary ways. But both are false. We are accustomed to moving within the structures which the Church has historically used to express itself, and which are so often accepted externally, even if it was not the Church itself which generated them. Yet the flow of life in the Spirit, passing through real people, is also able to generate forms and structures corresponding to the life the Spirit communicates, as happened with the liturgy and the sacraments. It is not a question of defending or skipping over forms, but of encouraging the Church to generate, in the Spirit, its own way of assembling, organizing, structuring itself which is more in accordance with what it is – its trinitarian mode of existence communicated to human beings.

We are experiencing enormous difficulties in areas where the Church has been for centuries, precisely because of this structural and organizational setup. But we do not manage to ask ourselves what the Spirit is telling us through historical events, and we simply go ahead trying to patch up the holes, combine parishes, set up pastoral groups, all the while consoling ourselves that in some places where the so-called 'young churches' are, parishes are still flourishing, novitiates are not falling in numbers and Catholic schools are full. It is as if we are unable to understand that earlier on it was like that among us too. It is as if we did not know how to learn the lessons of history.

Central Eastern Europe is an eloquent example. Under communism the Church had lost practically all its works, its structures were reduced to a minimum when it was not confined to being a clandestine Church. Yet the Church carried out an enormous pastoral activity and Christians enjoyed great respect among the people precisely because of their witness of faith. When communism fell, there was a lack of any theological, wisdom-based interpretation of what God had given and said over those decades that could be a spiritual treasure both for the Churches of the East and a gift they could offer to the Churches in the rest of the world. Saint John Paul II even called a European Synod with this in mind, but what we expected of it did not occur. As soon as it was in a position to do so, the Church in these parts immediately sought to recover everything it had lost: the previous style, institutions, properties ... And now we practically find ourselves amid the same spiritual, ecclesial, theological poverty as the rest of Europe.

4. *The shift toward communion*

If we try to list some of the fundamental directions of Vatican II's teaching, one is certainly that of no longer identifying the Church as being structured like a para-State or even para-Empire, but with the people of God on the move toward the kingdom, toward the communion of the Father, Son and Spirit. That was only the beginning of a radical rethinking of the Church that nevertheless was not brought to a conclusion in any developed and profound way.

Although part of history, so made up of men and women belonging to specific times and cultures, the Church is at the same time in a continual *exodus*, incessantly on the move toward the goal of its fulfilment. The Church is this people on the move as communion within the body of Christ. The only reality on which it is based as it goes ahead, is its ontological structure, that is, its life as communion. The

Church of Vatican II rediscovered its identity as Church-in-communion, hence synodal. It is clear, then, that the way for it to be governed needs to be radically rethought from this identity, such that its structure can be an icon of its ontological truth. But we are just at the beginnings of developing the whole process needed for this rethinking. By moving among the peoples, the Church will attract through its way of being and existing. It is life as communion which attracts because this kind of life is a manifestation of beauty.

It is a Church that becomes a neighbour to everyone, where that neighbourliness is an intrinsic category of a people on the move, Church as communion. It does not mean individuals who come together and walk together, but humanity in Christ receiving the gift of life as communion from the Holy Spirit. Life as communion is achieved through love. It is love as the gift of the Holy Spirit which creates a communal existence, a place where love is realized. And love attracts.[7] The life of the baptized as an open community which allows itself to be challenged, and which is involved[8] because it is creative, because free, because it is communion, is the only truly convincing reality of our proclamation.[9]

Clearly, in such a setup, there is the echo of a rediscovered and more vital, existential, trinitarian theology, a rediscovered freshness of the person as an essential ecclesial

---

7 Cf. WILLIAM OF SAINT-THIERRY, *Speculum fidei*, 46 (*PL* 180, 384D).

8 Cf. FRANCIS, *Address to participants in the International Congress on Catechesis*, Paul VI Hall, 27 September 2013.

9 Cf. FRANCIS, *Homily at the Mass with bishops at the 37th*

and theological category for tackling the problem of the one and the many, the local and the universal Church. And it is around the person that everything else turns, viewed from the fresh but at the same time typical ancient perspective of the great Fathers – the whole missionary and evangelizing approach which means walking with the women and men and children of every age. It is a relational approach, a relational texture of friendship, a taking up of the burdens, pains and problems of our contemporaries. It is letting the people with whom we live see that the Church is going through what all of humankind is going through – the same anxieties, difficulties, problems, the same historical rough patches – but that at the same time it experiences all these things in a new way. And not because it has more powerful tools, greater and more influential works, but because of the life of Christ who shapes the mind and the life of Christians through his paschal experience. The Christian finds the nexus between the historical moment he or she is going through, and Christ's redemption. Everything finds its meaning in him, but it is the Holy Spirit who communicates it to us as something that belongs to us, that we perceive as our own, and that unites us with Christ and other human beings.

5. *From Constantine's throne to Peter's chair*

This is the framework Pope Francis fits into. Appearing on the balcony immediately after his election, he presented himself not as Pope but as the Bishop of Rome, and asked the people to pray for him or bless him. It was a gesture that

WYD, Cathedral of San Sebastiano, Rio de Janeiro, 27 July 2013.

carried considerable symbolic value In just a single instant he had announced that he would be changing the habitual structures, not by changing organizational charts but their very meaning. He immediately said that the pope is a bishop of a particular Church and therefore is close to his people. In an instant he brought down the distance that had characterized papal power for centuries. In an instant he had redesigned the scenario which great pastors and theologians of the early centuries had, where the gathered people welcome their bishop into their midst as one of the people given to the people, where the bishop sees himself as the head, but the head of the body as an expression of this body, and where the body is organically connected with the head. In an instant the path for the way forward had been taken. It took us back many centuries, before our cohabitation with Empire had provided the opportunity for confusing Peter's chair with Constantine's throne, as Bernard of Clairvaux wrote to Pope Eugene III.[10] In fact, Pope Francis chooses not to live in the palace and has recently removed his effigy from Vatican coins: another gesture replete with meaning.

The Pope is taking serious note of the fact that with Vatican II the model of a Constantinian, Theodosian Church is finished. But with it begins a transition of the whole ecclesial structure. When Francis continues to speak of a Church that 'goes forth',[11] of the frontier Church, a 'field hospital',[12] of pastors with the 'smell of the sheep' on

10 Cf. BERNARD OF CLAIRVAUX, *De consideratione*, IV, III (PL 182, 776A).
11 *EG*, 20.
12 Interview with *La Civiltà Cattolica*, 2013 III 461 | 3918

them,[13] when he says that 'time is greater than space',[14] these are all important messages for saying that the Holy Spirit is asking the Church for the courage to be itself, to abandon the categories we have absorbed over centuries of cohabitation with para-imperial, para-state structures. The State belongs to the natural order,[15] insofar as it is a work of human beings, while the Church is of the spiritual order because it receives its communal way of existing and living in Christ from the Holy Spirit. This difference is expressed in a masterful way by Berdjaev:

> It seems that the enigma of who the person is may be the most impenetrable of all for philosophical thinking, and the one that more than any other is in need of revelation, needs to be nurtured by revelation. Person is not, like the individual, a natural phenomenon, does not belong to the order of nature in an objectified world. Person is the image and likeness of God and exists only for this; it belongs to the order of the spirit and is revealed in the destiny of existence.[16]

(19 September 2013).

13 *Homily at the Chrism Mass*, 28 March 2013.

14 *EG*, 222-225.

15 'The family, as also the state, is not a spiritual phenomenon and is not situated on the plane of the Spirit': N. BERDYAEV, *The Meaning of the Creative Act*, Semantron Press; Reprint ed. edition (June 26, 2009), though the text is taken from the Italian translation, *Il senso della creazione*, (or. Russian, Moscow 1916) Jaca Book, Milan 1994, 264.

16 N BERDYAEV, *Solitude and Society*. London: Geoffrey Bles,

Here it is not about an opposition between the natural and the supernatural, already overcome by the ancient Fathers, but of an opposition between a vision of the human being which is merely psychosomatic, and hence of an existence locked into the individuality of one's own nature, and one which is of the person as a relational existence according to the communion of the Holy Spirit, therefore as a gift received, an agapaic and paschal existence. The Church is a body of communion of persons, that is, of identities who emerge through relationships.[17] Through baptism, the Christian receives a relational existence according to God, where the Other is the epicentre of relationship. In the Eucharist the entire Church is on a journey to experience relationship in a kind of ecstasy, a shift toward the kingdom where it finds its fulfilment. If person is realized through this going forth and out of oneself, for Pope Francis the Church too corresponds to this image where the other, in relationship, is the epicentre. The Church is the image of this humanity going forth, going out of itself, finding its epicentre in the Other, toward the kingdom of God. It is clear that this Other is God, but it passes through the other who is every human being.[18]

1938, and later reprints, though the text is taken from the Italian translation, *L'io e il mondo*, (or. Russian, Paris s.d.) Bompiani, Milan 1942, 204.

17 Cf. J ZIZIOULAS, *Communion and Otherness*, London-New York 2006, though the reference here is taken from the Italian edition, *Comunione e alterità*, Lipa, Rome 2016, 11.

18 Cf. FRANCIS, *Address to participants in the International Congress on Catechesis*, Paul VI Hall, 27 September 2013.

6. Starting out from the person, with the Trinity as background

The Pope comes from the spiritual tradition of Saint Ignatius Loyola who, in an era seeking to reform the Church which had become completely worldly, saw that one could not proceed with clear and distinct ideas, but by taking a spiritual path. Now, the spiritual path is always a personal one, and personal means ecclesial, because relational. Ignatius was certainly under the influence of the modern era, an era that has been at the height of the cultural triumph of the individual, of humanism. But it is interesting that, by contrast with Luther – both men on a profound spiritual path – it was right at the end of his spiritual search at La Storta that Ignatius discovered the great trap that the individual is, and understood that spiritual experience, that is, the experience of redemption in Christ, can only be personal, meaning relational. If I have encountered Christ and the Holy Spirit has given me his life, if I have been redeemed, I am no longer an individual existence but a personal, an ecclesial one. Ignatius discovered that the spiritual journey of the person coincides with the Church, is inseparable from ecclesial convergence.[19]

---

19 In his Autobiography, no. 96., Ignatius states: "[the pilgrim] saw so clearly that God the Father placed him with Christ His Son, that he did not dare to doubt it" (taken from the Project Gutenberg online edition, the reference being to p. 141 of the 1900 Benzinger, New York edition , ed. JFX O'Conor SJ). Gradually Ignatius understood that this meant his service to the Church as obedience to the Pontiff. Cf. *Formule dell'Istituto della Compagnia di Gesù*, n. 1 (in *Gli scritti di Ignazio di Loyola*, 215) and G.

Francis comes from this tradition in which, at the beginning of the *Spiritual Exercises*, Ignatius suggests to the one guiding them that he be careful not to begin from things in general, but from the person, from where the person is actually at, from his or her situation, and see how the Spirit is acting in this person, how he wants to encounter the person, how he is knocking at the heart so that the person opens up to the Lord's action.[20]

The task of the one giving the Exercises is to accompany each person on this journey. Once they have come to this encounter with the Lord it will be the Holy Spirit who will guide them. Ignatius trusts strongly in the maturity of the Christian after the encounter with the Saviour. The true theologian has this prophetic outlook on humanity and therefore today, theologizing is especially knowing how to discern, knowing how to recognize where the Spirit is acting in humanity, and what steps this new life demands be taken for it to be realized in history.

Francis has immediately let us see that this is his approach. This is also the great novelty of his Apostolic Exhortation, *Amoris Laetitia*, which touches on a huge problem within the Church. Courageously, the Pope proposes a comprehensive approach within which one immediately notices the background of trinitarian personalism, where we cannot at the moment tackle such a serious and complex problem as

---

DUMEIGE, "Visión de La Storta. Historia y Espiritualidad", *Centro Ignaziano di Spiritualità* 57 (1988) 13-64.

20   Cf., IGNATIUS OF LOYOLA, *Spiritual Exercises*, notes 2a, 6a, 7a, 8a, 10a, 14a, 15a, 17a and especially 18a, 19a and 20a.

lies at the heart of this document with declarations, but by approaching things case by case, person by person, lovingly. When the time of transition has passed, and when we arrive at a living Church of Christians who are not nominalists but aware that they are living a life according to the Spirit, the problem will take care of itself, will no longer exist. At the moment we have a good number of people who find themselves bound by a sacramental bond without a conscious ecclesial life, without a true life in the Spirit. It is only possible to follow the Lord as he himself said: 'Those who love me will keep my word" (Jn 14:23). Francis wants a Church among the people which touches people lovingly, because someone who is touched by love will sooner or later discover the Countenance of this love.

So the plan of this pontificate begins to reveal itself. One model of Church is over, finished, and Francis has set out decisively toward a Church of people, a Church of communion, moving through history toward the full communion of which it is the 'sign and instrument'.[21] A Church made up of persons and not roles and powers, decidedly free of a mentality according to nature. A Church, then, where persons live for the faith, meaning they allow themselves to be transformed according to the manner of existence of communion, according to the trinitarian truth engraved on the human heart, the heart of the human being made in the image and likeness of God. These people will not exchange faith for ideology and religion, both

21 *Lumen Gentium (LG)* 1.

manifestations of the impulse to preserve themselves as individuals.[22] A Church no longer with ministers weighed down by mentalities and forms typical of natural categories – status, prestige, importance – like priests of any religion.

Francis is pulling the Church out of a situation where it has stalled, is dependent on its positions and structures – which are not in the order of life according to God, but according to this world – to direct it to a reality where its true face emerges, its true nature, which is essentially a spiritual one. In the homily he gave for the canonization of John XXIII and John Paul II, he stressed how these pontiffs had already cooperated 'in renewing and updating the Church in keeping with her pristine features.'[23] Francis is decisively shifting the Church toward the new creation, toward the fullness of communion in Christ, toward the manifestation of its true nature which is spiritual and not a parallel society living according to improved natural social forms. A Church which is a parallel society, when and if it truly did succeed in bettering the natural forms of human coexistence, would still not express a new mode of being. It would only be an attempt to lift natural things to a higher level. But in a reality of this kind it could still continue to live with a worldly mentality and way of acting, with a self-affirming will typical of the individual, and indeed of individualism.

---

22   Cf. CH YANNARIS, *Contro la religione*, (or. Greek, Athens 2006) Qiqajon, Magnano 2012.
23   FRANCIS, *Homily for the Mass of Canonization of Blessed John XXII and John Paul II*, 27 April 2014.

Because of all this there is a need for a way of theologizing to emerge that is at the service of the Church at this historical moment. True theology has always been pastoral because it has always had the Truth at heart as the Truth that saves and transforms. The greatest theologians have also been pastors and the greatest pastors have made us see their theological vision through their care for the Christian community. Therefore we are always dealing with a systematic, comprehensive vision which holds life, care for people, problems that arise, and seeking what the Spirit is saying to the Church, together. There is a need for a theology to emerge that has the salvation of the people at heart, that is truly spiritual, and that helps the people of God to recognize the shift from a way of thinking which is rooted in a natural mentality, to one which is truly according to Christ, according to the gift of life received. We are certainly talking about a theology which is part of the grand wisdom stream of the tradition and which is not just limited to our Church now but breathes through centuries and spaces. Since in this effort to bring the Church into a new era, Francis finds a great consensus in Churches of other traditions as well,[24] it is an intrinsically ecumenical one because all Churches see the need to free themselves from a model we have felt at home in for centuries but which has almost brought us to our death, and which the Spirit is asking us to leave behind.

24 There are already many letters and statements from Patriarchs of the Orthodox Churches or from the Archbishop of Canterbury expressing a common vision with Pope Francis, and sometimes these are followed up with common gestures. For the most recent common gestures cf. *Irénikon*, LXXXIX (2016), nos.

In this text, following the example of Abram's call, where he was called to leave his home and country behind, we will attempt to untangle the passages of a spiritual theology which tries to enter into this reasoning process of Pope Francis in order to envisage a view no longer tied to a past structure but inspired by the very mystery of the Church, by Christ and the Holy Spirit.

And since the beauty of liturgy is a springboard for evangelization, as Pope Francis says,[25] we will try to show that the existence of the Christian and the Church is steeped in the liturgy from which the Christian and the Church lives and which creates the scenario for a systematic, comprehensive approach, a communal one typical of the life received and based on its origins and its trinitarian destination.

2-4, 161-162.
25 *EG*, 24.

Chapter I
A NOTE ON TERMINOLOGY

1. Terms

Before actually starting out on our theme, there is a need for some clarification.

Spiritual theology is that area of theology which deals with the dynamics and processes of spiritual life in our Christian living. It embraces all of theology which it interprets from the perspective of the spiritual life, or the believer's appropriation of it. But since the theological discipline which today bears the name 'spiritual theology' has not always existed, and its content, method, and relationship with the other theological disciplines has changed, it would be good, as we set out, to offer a basic summary of these changes and then give a brief description of the meaning which will be given to the terms used in this text.

Spiritual. The adjective 'spiritual' is a creation of Latin-speaking Christians.[1] While concrete things in Christian life were often called by the name they already had (baptism, for example, had been adopted from the Greek – *baptisma*), abstract ideas were given a Latin expression. *Spiritualis* comes from the context of the translation of Paul's word pair *sarx-pneuma.* This word pair 'flesh-spirit' (*caro-spiritus*)

---

1 Cf. CH MOHRMANN, *Études sur le latin des chrétiens*, II, Edizioni di Storia e Letteratura, Rome 1961, 105.

gives rise to a specifically Christian set of terms: *carnalis, spirit(u)alis, carnaliter, spirit(u)aliter*.[2]

The fact that the adjective *spiritualis* enters Latin as a translation of the Greek *pneumatikos* from the Pauline Letters, generally a word in Paul which is tied to the *Pneuma* of God, tells us that it had something to do with the Holy Spirit from the outset.[3]

Also *spiritualis* very soon appears with this meaning as a noun ('the spiritual').

Spirituality. The word 'spirituality' is very rare prior to the 13th century, a time when it begins to be used but whose use remains rather rare in authors like Bernard of Clairvaux or Hugo and Richard of Saint Victor, who prefer abstract composite terms using the adjective *spiritualis*, the adverb *spiritualiter* or the noun *spiritus*, which have the merit of remaining anchored in real, concrete life.[4]

---

2   Cf. ID., *Études sur le latin des chrétiens*, II, Edizioni di Storia e Letteratura, Rome 1958, 24-5, 89; III Rome 1965, 104, 115, IV, Rome 1977, 14.

3   The 26 occurrences of *pneumatikos* in the NT clearly have different shades of meaning, but taken as a whole, what I have said still applies. 'The divine action which the Greek Bible designates with the word *pneuma* is explicit, and much more decisively at the moment the awaited salvation is realized. In fact Jesus revealed to us the strict relationship of this saving action of God with the third Person of the Trinity, the Holy Spirit ... Everything in the NT, therefore, appeared in strict relationship with the divine *pneuma*; that is, it was described as being *pneumatikos*'; P DACQUINO, *"L'aggettivo «spiritualis» nei testi liturgici"*, *Rivista Biblica* XV (1967) 275-279, here 276. Cf. G BARBAGLIO, *La prima lettera ai Corinzi, Introduzione, versione, commento*, Scritti delle origini cristiane 16, EDB, Bologna 1995, 179.

4   Cf. S SOLIGNAC, *Spiritualité. I. Le mot et l'histoire*, in *DS* 14

Beginning with the 17th century, the word begins to spread widely through all European languages to indicate the way of conceiving existence on the basis of the religious circumstances of a person or group. In the 19th century, following changes in cultural sensitivity, 'spirituality' was more likely to stress the aspect of the realization (rather than the conceiving) of a way of living and its adaptation to historical conditions, in order to recover a concrete and existential dimension.

Spiritual theology. Beginning with the 1960s, having by now achieved full citizenship in theological vocabulary, the word *spirituality* gave rise to an abundance of studies which tried to define the proper nature of 'spiritual theology', also called the 'theology of spirituality'. Research developed in two directions; questions as to: a) the meaning of *spirituality* and hence of spiritual theology; b) the place of spiritual theology among all the theological disciplines.[5]

How had these questions been answered previously? In a certain sense one could say that treatises on the spiritual life had made their appearance very early in the history of Christianity. Beside works of a more speculative nature which were aimed at exploring dogma or defending against heresies, some writings very soon appeared which were aimed at nurturing the life of faith: from Clement's *Pedagogue* to Origen's treatise on prayer, to the works of Evagarius, to the *Life of St Anthony* ... and it is this last-named work which reveals the relationship that existed in the ancient Church

(1900), 1144.
    5 Cf. *Ibidem*, 1150.

between the understanding of the faith and the life of faith. Its author, Athanasius, gives his main character the title of 'man of God' because he considered him to be an example of what Christian perfection means, identified as it is with divinization. Anthony is the personal manifestation of the famous formula defended by Athanasius in the dogmatic area: 'The word of God became man so that we might become God.'[6] This mutual fusion between theology and the spiritual life was considered to be not only the very condition for holiness, but also for theology, given that the practice of theology was conceived of only in its personal relationship with the *Theos* – the Father – through the *Logos* – Christ – in the Spirit. Theology was considered to be a *gnōsis*-wisdom that leads not only to an intellectual understanding, but transfigures the whole human being throughout his or her life.

This outlook changes radically once the scholastics come along, when theological thinking shifts from the context of Church to University. This meant theology found itself separated from spiritual life, liturgy, ministry etc. The thinking was that this separation of scholastic theology from the spiritual life could be remedied by adding teaching aimed at motivating the 'affections'. Thus, during the 18th century, treatises classified under the title of 'ascetic and mystical

---

6   Athanasius of Alexandria, *L'incarnazione del Verbo* 54, 3 (PL 25, 192; SC 199, 458). Cf. T. ŠPIDLÍK – M. TENACE – R. ČEMUS, *Il monachesimo secondo la tradizione dell'oriente cristiano*, (or. Fr., Rome 1999) Lipa, Rome 2007, 29. Note: Athanasius text *The Incarnation of the Word*, is readily available online in English: https://www.ccel.org/ccel/athanasius/incarnation.html.

theology' came into being, which would give life to a new specialization in theology.[7] From this perspective, 'ascetics' would be a study of 'ordinary perfection' which assumes voluntary ascetical effort, a human exercise (*askēsis*), while 'mystical' referred to 'extraordinary perfection', an exclusive initiative of God.[8]

At the end of the 19th and beginning of the 20th centuries, 'spiritual theology' was added as a supplementary chapter to dogmatic and moral theology, focusing on the experiential, personal dimension, not the conceptual dimension of faith. Pius IX, in his Constitution *Deus Scientiarum Dominus* on 24 May 1931, established a specialized chair in Faculties of Theology to teach ascetics as an 'auxiliary discipline', while mystical theology was designated as a 'special discipline'. Thus for the first time, ascetics became a subject in a program of studies envisaged by the universal Church. It was optional, so considered secondary, since it did not enjoy a high reputation, so much so that it had to be recommended

---

[7] The term *mystical theology* goes back a long way. It can already be found in writings of the Areopagite. But here it does not point to something coming from ordinary experience. On the contrary, if *mystikos* comes from the verb *myō*, which is the root form of the word *mystērion*, with which the ancient Church pointed to the experiences of baptism and eucharist, 'mystical' was what characterized all its members. This meaning is still maintained by the Orthodox Churches, where mystical experience means personally experiencing the content of the common faith. Cf. V Lossky, *La teologia mistica della Chiesa d'Oriente*, (or. Fr., Paris 1944) EDB, Bologna 1985, 4.

[8] Cf. J De Guibert, *La plus ancienne « théologie ascétique »*, in *Revue d'ascétique et de mystique*, 17 (1937) 404-408.

by some authority.[9] Tied to this teaching was the production of scholastic manuals. Another problem arose at the same time, one of methodology: what was the method proper to this 'theology' and how did it relate to the other theological disciplines and, more immediately, with moral theology?

On the eve of the Second Vatican Council, many parties expressed the desire to recover a theological vision whereby the different disciplines would be considered within an overall experiential framework of the gnostic-sapiential kind, with a biblical and patristic foundation and open to contemporary culture. On the basis of the renewal of theology, the object of spiritual theology was identified in Christian life as the spiritual life, life according to the Spirit. This is distinct, on the one hand, from the dogmatic discourse of theological anthropology and, on the other, from moral discourse. Since in recent decades specialization in theology has led the theologian to appeal to auxiliary sciences to the point where such disciplines with their technical side have ended up playing a much greater role in research and teaching,[10] spiritual theology too has become ever more dependent on the results of the psychological sciences and other human sciences. Hence the need to once more specify the content and method of spiritual theology in its relationship to the content of faith as embodied in life in all its aspects.

9 This is testified to by the many interventions of the Congregation for Catholic Education on the matter.
10 M Dupuy, *La notion de spiritualité*, in *DS* 14 (1900), 1166-7.

2. The sense in which we speak of 'spiritual theology' in this book

The fundamental factor we cannot ignore is that the term 'spiritual' finds its *raison d'être* and hence its meaning as well, in the Holy Spirit. We cannot use terms like 'spiritual' (both as adjective and noun), or 'spirituality' without a direct connection with the Holy Spirit. The basis for any understanding of 'spiritual' or 'spirituality' is the gift of the Holy Spirit whom the Father sends *in* and *by means of* his Son. And since, in the Christian tradition, the Holy Spirit is the Lord of the *koinōnia*, the living and personal bond which unites the Father with his Son and with us,[11] sons and daughters in the Son, 'spiritual' indicates everything that opens, leads to, relates the human being to God as Father. Hence the term 'spiritual' always points to a communal, relational and thus personal reality. It can never be confused with something merely intellectual, a kind of analogy, or the indication of some supernatural energy the individual acquires through personal effort. By 'spiritual', then, we mean everything that unites the human being with God through the Holy Spirit's activity in a relationship which is not just any relationship but one of children to parent, thus making us brothers and sisters. And since the Holy Spirit is the Lord who gives life, the 'spiritual', also as an adjective,

---

11 A Russian theologian, Sergei Bulgakov, quoting *Jn* 16:32: 'I am not alone because the Father is with me' – says that the 'with' which unites the Father with the Son is 'a cryptogram, a hidden name for the Holy Spirit': S BULGAKOV, *Il Paraclito*, (or. Russian, Paris 1936) EDB, Bologna 1987, 446.

concerns all the dimensions of existence in which life opens up to a Countenance, or comes from a Countenance and reveals it, and strengthens life as communion, as relationship. Every reality – be it with the cosmos or with history – then becomes spiritual in opening the human heart to the action of the Spirit who reveals the meaning and truth of things and events.

The emphasis in the noun 'spirituality' is evidently more on its realization, that is, the full acknowledgement of the life of the Holy Spirit, of the gift of the Father which reaches us through the Son. 'Spirituality', then, because it puts the emphasis more on the realization, manifestation and fulfilment of the life of the Holy Spirit in humanity, in real people, in places and history, highlights the way this acknowledgement and its manifestation takes place, or the way in which the human being becomes a spiritual being, a creative being, open to the gift of the Spirit. The human being becomes a manifestation of the transfiguration of humanity in the person of Christ, in his Body. Therefore, the way we allow ourselves to be transfigured, and allow the gift we have acknowledged to transform us, can be called 'spirituality'.

This acknowledgement of the gift, and being open to transfiguration, is realized in various ways. There is a great plurality about it, guaranteed by the Holy Spirit, but at the same time there is a consolidated unity because transfiguration brings about our identity as a part of Christ, as a member of his Body, which is persons who belong to a people journeying in sonship with him and this becomes our life. We can also observe some of the expressions of spirituality in the way in which we are hidden with Christ – who is our life (cf. Col 3:4).

If 'spirituality' is the way the spiritual is realized, does this mean that some of the recurring expressions today, such as 'Buddhist spirituality' or the spirituality of other religions, are legitimate? We believe so, and that it is possible to speak in these terms precisely because spirituality includes within itself the manner of transformation that occurs through its acceptance. For us Christians the *manner* indicates *acceptance of the gift and the creative activity which is already taking place through this acceptance*, and then through the ever more complete integration of all of human existence in this gift which is the life of the Holy Spirit and our belonging to Christ's humanity. In the majority of the religions we know about, instead, the manner tends more to a realization of the religious pattern, the religious journey very much bound up with human effort, with the asceticism with which the human being reaches out to a higher universe. Despite this profound difference, we can correctly call this 'spirituality' because of the Holy Spirit who blows where he chooses (cf. Jn 3:8), readies human nature to share in the divine life and act according to the inspirations he arouses. In the end, it is recognized through active charity, in experience as an expression of self-gift, as peace, motivation for creative, inclusive encounter. The 'spirituality' of a religion marked by a life of charity, openness, acceptance of the other, by peaceful gestures when encountering the other, can then be called such by our spiritual theology too. What is really important is whether the spirituality points to a way of living one's humanity as charity, acceptance, or in other words the categories of life of the Spirit who moves us to live according to the Son. We can observe features of the life lived by the Son of God in this life, even if the person concerned does not mention his name because he still does not know about him. This is also true for us Christians, given that it is not enough to just appeal to a proclaimed faith: we will all be judged on love.

By 'spiritual theology' – perhaps the most problematic term in our Latin tradition – we mean first of all the manner of theologizing which proceeds from life in the Spirit. So, it is a manner which characterizes any Christian theology, whatever its object – because spiritual theology shows that every theology comes from the gift of the Holy Spirit, from life in Christ, from sharing in trinitarian life. Spiritual theology is the condition for any theological study, with its dimension of unity between the contents of theology and the life of the Church, meaning the communal existence of the baptized, those who are grafted onto Christ. Spiritual theology has a communal dimension *par excellence*, because it studies the way in which the human being converges with the action of the Holy Spirit, and how he or she remains in Christ Jesus; it studies how the paschal transfiguration process in humanity comes about, how the human person is transfigured according to a relational, filial mentality in the different dimensions of real life. A spiritual theology, then, is understood as the proper manner for any theologizing, because it is attentive to the unity between life and thought, faith as content (*fides quae*) and faith as attitude (*fides qua*), as relationship.

If we accept this meaning, one could also believe that spiritual theology no longer makes sense in a new way of structuring theology where the wisdom aspect is given more emphasis. Going back through history we have seen how it arose as a discipline right at the time theology became fragmented, no longer developing as one body of study but dividing into a range of branches which followed different methodologies. We believe, nevertheless, that spiritual theology is also called to exist within a more systematic and comprehensive vision of theology, because it expresses the mentality needed by every believer to realize the new life in the many dimensions of real life, as an expression of the new creation, according to the eschatological dimension.

3. *The method*

What has been said is enough to indicate that the method of spiritual theology cannot consist in isolating the object of its study. We are talking about precisely the opposite to this. Spiritual theology's method is a *symbolic* method, in the sense of the first Christian era where the symbol was a way of looking at reality inscribed in creation brought about by the Word, and brought to fulfilment in the Incarnation of Christ. It looked at how the Son of God is present in Jesus of Nazareth, how every phenomenon displays something more profound and real within it than it can do just on its own. So even the verification of thinking is not to be found within the language schemes it is expressed in. The understanding gained from experience is signified and communicated through language but never exhaustively through linguistic formation. One must go back to the depth of the experience, which is one of communion.[12] Here, life and thought are part of an unceasing dynamic, in an organic relationship, and where within the one reality, one constantly discovers the other. Indeed, an understanding of the unity of two worlds – the created and the uncreated – is the fulfilment of the spiritual because it means discovering oneself in the relationship with Christ in whose divinity and humanity [the Italian original calls it *divinoumanità*] unity is fulfilled. Therefore the method is characterized as one of ecclesial communion, meaning it is the expression of being interwoven within the Church as the Body of the Son.

Spiritual theology, like its method, creates the condition which even today is only glimpsed with difficulty, whereby understanding deepens our faith because it deepens our communion with Christ and those who are of Christ. And not just this. Because it is detached from the more analytical and defined categories, it is the theology *par excellence* for dialogue with people outside the Church. Thanks to its predominantly symbolic and hence inclusive and relational approach, it does not prioritize one dimension of the human being over another – for example thinking, ideas, science, ethics – but seeks to take the human being as a whole. Thus,

---

12 Cf. Ch Yannaras, *Relational Ontology*, Holy Cross Orthodox Press (September 30, 2011), though the text here is taken from the Italian translation, *Ontologia della relazione*, (or. Greek, Athens 2004), Città Aperta, Troina 2004, 19.

after having seen the poor results of a fundamental theology which pursued its dialogue with the world at a primarily apologetic, argumentative level based on concepts and reasoning, in the future, spiritual theology could play a very significant role for the Church's mission in the world.[13]

4. *The sources of spiritual theology*

If the method of spiritual theology is one typical of the Holy Spirit, the weaving of a relational network between the particular and the whole, the individual and the collective, the one and the all, then the source of spiritual theology is the Church's experience. It is not possible to theologize in any genuine way when locked into the experience of just one Church, just one era, just one type of cultural experience, because of itself the Church – inasmuch as it is *ekklēsia*, synapsis (σύναξις), a meeting among those who have understood the call – it is an original event of communion and unity. A Church – that is, a local Church or also a Church of apostolic tradition that seeks to be universal – because it claims this title, must be in communion with the other apostolic traditions. Hence spiritual method means thinking with others both in time and place, so that the true manner of reasoning is already marked by the 'eighth day' or the communion of times and places.

The Church's experience is the experience of new life, of the human being who lives life in the Holy Spirit. Talking about sources must also be woven into the method

---

13 As an example of such an approach, cf. V TRUHLAR, *Lessico di spiritualità*, Queriniana, Brescia 1973.

of spiritual theology because in this case, too, it is about acknowledgement, acceptance on the part of the human being. Therefore the method consist of openness and acceptance. The way for theological thinking to proceed is not to begin from the human being as such but from the encounter that unlocks the human being's readiness to accept the gift of life in the Holy Spirit. This encounter is the result of the paschal mystery. In fact it is necessary that a life destined to die achieves this death, that the cycle is complete, so that it can make way for a new life in such a way that it pervades all of human reality with its newness. This means that the method safeguards a predominantly contemplative attitude. This process of welcoming life through the death and resurrection of another life – new life – coincides with the paschal mystery which the human being experiences in baptism. This is why the sources of spiritual theology are found in the Church's experience, the new life of the new creation, and the presence, *parousia*, of the kingdom.

Today, after decades of subjectivism, perhaps we are afraid of the word 'experience'. But for the ancients, it meant the direct understanding of the passing through death to a new reality, never before imagined, because it is marked by a communal life. An *understanding*, then, which gave rise also to a different *consciousness*, a *consciousness of self in communion*. Life awakens, becomes conscious, and I have 'experience' through relationship: *tu es, ergo sum* (you are, therefore I am). The individual self is dead, and another self in Christ arises which is not a simple replacement for the old self but a new way of existence of my self, which becomes conscious of itself by relating as son (or daughter) to the Father. We have this experience when we are personally integrated with Christ's unique pasch, which takes place in the Church, the place where the Risen Lord lives. In this pasch or passage, the individual self dies and a communal self rises. The baptized person begins to live in Christ and is grafted onto a typically divine existence: 'I am in the Father and the Father is in me' (Jn 14:10).

We rise to this new life through baptism, take note of it in our personal consciousness – a relational, no longer an individual one – and seek to express it and develop it creatively according to a new understanding, a new way of feeling, wanting, because now all this is filial, of Christ, but is mine at the same time.

It is in this context of the dynamic between life and creativity, life and new understanding, that inspiration is located, the source and object of spiritual theology. Therefore spiritual theology purifies every theological method, given that the new life cannot be poured into old vessels (cf. Mt 9:17) and that Christ's love surpasses every understanding (cf. Eph 3:19). There is a need to be creative because we are called to say spiritual things in spiritual terms and thus involve all of language, the entire cultural sphere of the person in this new way of living and thinking.

Since the Church's experience has its origin in the Easter event, in constantly seeing the Risen Lord rising in the community of believers, the mystery of the Church is the mystery of the Risen Lord who is alive in history. But since this experience has its origins in the Easter passing over, spiritual theology cannot but consider the entire process as the source and object of its theologizing. There is a need, then, to begin first of all from the concrete situation of the human being, from how this human being is born into circumstances marked by sin, until the transfiguration that takes place in such a life through death and in the resurrection to life with Christ. Spiritual theology must consider the entire paschal process of the human being from a spiritual point of view.

The source and object of spiritual theology's research will secondly be also the way in which openness takes place, the beginning of the convergence with God's action, conversion, acceptance of the gift. The source and object of spiritual theology's research, finally, will be the death of one life and the regeneration of another, that can no longer be in the manner of an individual but which is necessarily an ecclesial, communal existence. It takes place through the work of the Church in a sacramental event – the so-called sacraments of Christian initiation: Baptism, Confirmation and Eucharist.

5. *A spiritual outlook on humanity in all its complexity*

The first dimension of research concerns an individual existence still, the second a dramatic, paschal passage through death, and the third the birth of the person in a theological sense.

In the first dimension the great activity is renunciation, recognizing oneself in all humility, admitting one's finiteness, so it is a submission to the other, to a certain mortification of the individual self which begins to recognize its limitations.

This is already a first step which is an initiation into the openness and obedience which lead to acceptance. It was in obedience that the Son was born, an obedience that is discovered at a concrete moment, but certainly one that also constitutes an ongoing character of love.

The second dimension is characterized by the acceptance of death due to the relationship which reveals a different meaning of existence. Taking account of the other already begins to take precedence; we already trust that the gift is greater than death and have the inner conviction that we can recognize love only when the wish to be deserving of love dies in us completely. Death is the complete inactivity of the will to be self-affirming, and the result of faith being activated, that is, accpetance of and trust in the other.

The third dimension is the creativity that begins with the acceptance of a manner of personal existence, a relational one where the whole of the human reality – even that part of it most easily subject to the self-affirming will of the individual understanding which is not able to make room for the mystery of love – is absorbed in a personal existence. It is here that a new dimension of love is discovered: freedom, free belonging, which in turn generates a free creativity. Freedom is what love consists of in its essence. There is nothing necessary in love, so it is not the laws of nature which carry weight in love, with rules knowable through reason and therefore somehow subject to necessity. Instead it is the existence received from God which makes the self able to take possession of its own nature in a free way, able to live according to love, according to the gift. This new existence is exquisitely spiritual because it is acceptance of the gift of the Holy Spirit, of the gift of life as *koinōnia*, as love, the gift of life according to the paschal mystery, which is the way in which God's love lives within humanity in history. This is how Christ lived as the Son of God and true Man and this is how we are regenerated in the baptismal passage from one existence to another. The baptismal model, then, is the model for the Christian.

So spiritual theology must begin with the phenomenon of the human being as such. But since it is not tackling it from the ideological or moral and ethical point of view, or according to some precise methodology proper to contemporary culture, but dealing with it in a spiritual way – seeing how the Holy Spirit acts within it – it addresses itself to the human being with this attention. Spiritual theology turns to the human being by trying to grasp how the Holy Spirit is active within him or her, looks for the way through for life, reveals the way for new life in the human heart.

If spiritual theology is to begin from the actual situation of the human being, at the same time it cannot consider human beings according to the criteria of their culture, so it needs to bring other criteria into play – 'spiritual' ones – for the baptized person. According to the expression Paul uses in 1 Cor 2:13 (*'interpreting spiritual things in spiritual language'*), spiritual theology cannot consider the natural human being in terms of a natural wisdom, and the spiritual being in terms of a spiritual wisdom, given that the spiritual being is called to consider everything from a spiritual point of view (*'Those who are spiritual discern all things'*: 1 Cor

2:15). It is about having a spiritual outlook on the human being as such, in all his or her real concreteness. But how do we do this?

To overcome this dualism, earlier we encompassed everything in a kind of metaphysics which was the framework theology made use of. In a metaphysical system, the outlook on humanity is willy-nilly conditioned by a certain idealism and we try to overcome the non-correspondence of the human reality to an ideal plan which can also be understood as the Creator's plan for humanity, by being committed to and planning for improving the human situation. This way of proceeding, though, does not succeed in avoiding the dualist trap, because we are still working with the real-unreal pair and as a consequence, moralism and voluntarism are inevitable. History confirms this dualism: at a certain moment, by abandoning the metaphysical approach, reference to abstract principles, we moved on to interpreting the human situation by beginning from the approach suggested by the auxiliary sciences, which start from consideration of the human being as such. So we found ourselves back on the other side of the pendulum's swing. But this too is a misleading situation, and the deception consists of the fact that both approaches depend on the growth of the natural human being who should painlessly slip to a higher level of life. In recent decades, where the dominant approach was generally a socio-psychological one, the breakthrough to faith did not happen because there continued to be misunderstandings no less harmful than the metaphysical and moralistic spiritualisms of the past. In fact we cannot deal in a truthful and effective way with things of the Spirit using scientific or philosophical language and ways of thinking, given that the sciences themselves warn us that the action of the Holy Spirit and divine-human synergy are not the object of their study. So it is not possible to interpret the human phenomenon on the basis of the sciences, idealism, philosophical ethics, whatever school of psychology, and then put a spiritual-theological cover over it later.

6. *'Through the eyes of faith'*[14]

On this point there is a need to seriously consider Berdyaev's statement quoted in the introduction, when he says that the individual is of the natural order, so rationally accessible, while the person is of the spiritual order and therefore escapes rational understanding. It is precisely the outcome of life to clarify this difference. The individual comes to an end in a tragic split: on the one hand its bodily side has to admit that death is stronger; idealistically, according to a classic mode of thought, its ideal world, its values, can survive, but the identity of the ego or self cannot. Yet the destiny of the person is to become ever more whole and complete until it reaches its fulfilment in the *eschaton*, where communion will be the total identity of the ego, the self. And since the person is born of resurrection, it is the transfiguration wrought by the resurrection which is its foundational characteristic, a characteristic nevertheless

---

14 Cf. M TENACE, *Da* Gli occhi di fede *di Pierre Rousselot a Papa Francesco*, *Gregorianum* 96 (2015), no. 4, 679-687.

absolutely elusive for any method that deals with *individual* human nature. So a theology based on reasoning according to nature, like the methods of the modern sciences or the typical rational projections of various metaphysics, is unable to grasp the *event of the person itself*, that is, the mystery constituting it due to the love and freedom that characterizes its becoming – identity as communion which integrally involves the personal consciousness of the self, a luminous consciousness because it is a filial one.

Things being the way they are, it is only the action of the Holy Spirit (love) in the spiritual human being that succeeds in penetrating the opacity of individual nature, and also its resistance. It is only love, only a spiritual, agapaic understanding that can penetrate sin, death, isolation, separation and see the sense of it, because the way it does so is a symbolic way: in a separate reality, in a radically individual existence like the one sin has reduced the human being to, it already glimpses the One who took this reality upon Himself and in which it can overcome its mortal destiny to find itself in a luminous, communal existence. The symbol in fact is the unity of the two worlds which has come about only in Christ. While in the human being as such we see the tragedy of existence, our gaze is united with the gaze of the One who gave himself to this human existence, became man for this existence.

The authentic principle of evangelization and the Church's mission is also characterized by this approach. The Church's mission does not develop simply by noting the lack of correspondence of one reality with what could be an ideal, ethical, social or spiritual vision, but can only come from a communal vision, a unified one. A theological method that comes from an existence united to the life of Christ cannot be characterized by dualisms that it then tries to eliminate in various ways – or by cancelling from its perspective a problematic world marked by death, or by embracing an ideal universe. It is this method instead which becomes a way of thinking that makes us the place in which Christ loves this world marked by tragedy.

Today, theology finds itself isolated both from the life of the Church and the life of culture, including the culture it would like to be a contemporary one which suits the human being. It does not know how to make people fall in love, cannot release love, is unable to trigger the strength to live as a gift for those it would ideally like to be close to. In fact, in its desire to approach the natural human being, it does so by adopting a natural human mentality, and thus has difficulty in living in a radical way the new identity of the baptized, the new man, the christic, ecclesial self that can never be reconciled with the other mentality.

All this also helps us to grasp the impotence of theology faced with the precise tasks for which the Church needs its contribution. Indeed it is clear that approaches like the one just mentioned cannot contribute to developing a formation, a pedagogy, a journey of growth where individual human beings allow themselves to be transfigured by God's love in their humanity. It is a fact that by now, almost all the religious congregations and seminaries have come to observe the sterile formative value of these approaches, because the language, method, mentality that comes from them are not an explanation of new life, do not put in place a dynamic typical of ecclesial life. It is difficult, then, for a non-ecclesial mentality to encourage ecclesial formation.

If the model of this new existence is learned from being born to this new life – baptism – such an existence is realized and nourished in the Eucharist, which is the mystery of the Church. Therefore, a mentality and manner that does not draw from the Eucharistic structure will hardly bear fruit for the Church.

Chapter 2
HUMAN EXISTENCE CANNOT BE REDUCED TO ITS NATURE[1]

1. Escaping from death

The most frequent misunderstanding in our cultural context is to have the spiritual journey start from the identification of the concrete human being as created by God – good, successful, and indeed 'in his image and likeness' (cf. Gen 1:26). If we begin from this assumption and then look at the actual state of the human being we then have to confront the real human situation which seems to disavow this claim in almost every area of human existence.

Classical Greek thought is a response to such a way of reasoning, working on the basis of the individual-universal and real-ideal dynamic. Framed this way, 'spiritual' ends up meaning the ideal and the universal. The 'spiritual journey' then means the path the individual pursues to overcome his or her own individuality and enter into a universal dimension by realizing certain ideals. This applies mainly to the moral scene but not only that. And depending which cultural era one is in, it means emphasizing one or other value. But as we have seen, such an approach does not

---

1 Cf. T. Špidlík, *L'idea russa, un'altra visione dell'uomo*, (or. Fr., Troyes 1994) Lipa, Rome 1995, 26-28.

resolve the fundamental question of life, experienced all the more urgently when life encounters injury, suffering, death.

There are many ways of attempting to escape this disappearance into oblivion. Today, idealism or romanticism are certainly no longer in fashion. The preference today is more one of forgetting one's mortal state long before death reaches us. And so we see a strong cultural commitment, including a significant commercial outcome, to erasing all traces of this death in all the various ways it dots our existence. The entire history of humanity is a lengthy list of the many ways human beings have struggled with their selves to escape the question of death. But our culture today has discovered an approach that seems much more efficient: distraction, arousal of the senses which is so ongoing and invasive as to occupy the self's consciousness so radically that we forget who we are. It is obvious, then, that when the moment arrives when we have to finally accept that we are dying, we take every possible measure to prevent this happening. So all the ethical battles against euthanasia are destined to failure given that it is the mentality as a whole which cannot bear the question of our end and the limits of human existence. It is our culture that sees no other solution because it believes the truest, most ethical approach to tackling this circumstance is to forget it, distract oneself, not think about it.

The reality human beings find themselves in following their birth is to weep for their end, a tragedy we can already glimpse in the new-born's wailing.[2] This sad, intuitive

2   The Fathers claimed that tears came about after the fall.

observation which becomes ever more conscious over the years, is the drama of our existence. Everything beautiful, pleasurable that can cheer up life leaves a bitter aftertaste, a hint of the end, lurking in it. And this is not just because sooner or later this happy moment will pass, but because existence itself leads to tragedy. We can employ enormous energy and capital to distract us and not think about death, but this effort already in itself attests to the fact that death hangs over our existence like the sword of Damocles. The certainty of death as the outcome does not only ruin the enjoyment of life's most beautiful moments with the thought that they must come to an end, but much more seriously corrodes everything with its relativism, making a nonsense of everything the human being does to avoid it. As we see in two important Scriptural texts – Ecclesiastes 2 and Wisdom 2 – death makes everything relative. So much so that it is worth concluding: 'Let us eat and drink for tomorrow we die' (1 Cor 15:32). The fundamental question the human being has to tackle after birth, therefore, is the tragedy of our own existence. With this awareness, our life submits to absolute relativism. Everything we might do in a rush of goodness, love, joy and creativity is like a flower that withers and fades tomorrow, grass that will dry up sooner or later (cf. Is 40:6).

Cf. JOHN CHRYSOSTOM, *Le statue*, homily 11,3 (PG 49, 122). These homilies (e.g. On the Statues) are also available in English online, e.g. at http://www.newadvent.org/fathers/190103.htm

2. *If the will does not enter into sonship*

It is human existence as such which testifies to the gravity of the situation in which the consciousness of the self, the ego, is placed, a consciousness which nature weighs upon, and which this self has become a mere expression of. It is precisely human nature, inasmuch as it can be exalted, which keeps the ego in check. The ego can try to overcome nature's destiny – the grave – in two directions. Either upwards, through various metaphysical, philosophical, religious, ethical, romantic idealisms, or downwards, by abandoning itself to the passions, so that nature takes what it wants and the ego serves its instincts. In both cases, human nature dominates, using the ego to express itself through its will, but always with self-affirmation as the common denominator. In spite of this self-affirming ego that abuses all that is human, the human being perceives that the truth of existence does not all lie here, and another voice emerges within him or her. This is when we perceive that two inclinations coexist within us, the conflict of two wills both demanding satisfaction: one expressing our personal nature, the other manifesting the natural instinct opposed to the former, which has an impersonal face and leaves no room for our freedom. It is what Paul laments in Rom 7:15-25, when he says: '*Wretched man that I am! Who will rescue me from this body of death?*' (v. 24).

In fact, if there is no Christ to free us from this split between idealism or abandonment to our instincts, human existence cannot cross the wall that encloses us in our reality of death and oblivion. Nature cannot overcome itself. And the ego, the self, cannot ultimately heal nature, since it is reduced to one of its expressions and is subject to it. The will that lies in this wounded nature, poisoned by the sting of death, cannot become a healing will in the self, but only a deceptive one which suggests to reason the means and ends with which the self might apparently be saved. So reason, also being used by nature, cannot help but take off, using the momentum of the will, and then land tragically amid the observation of broken ideals. The 'human project' that has characterized our modern era does not solve the problem that the statue of Laocoön has already expressed, that is, that there is no salvation for the self if the body is not saved (fig. 1).

I do not need awareness if this is tied to my mortal existence. Such an awareness is of no use to me.

As we see in Géricault's *The Raft of the Medusa* (fig. 2) – where the survivors on the raft will not be able to wait for the ship visible on the horizon because by now rescue is a utopia and the character, who looks like the artist, is looking back as he pulls his dead son out of the water – the fate of a mindset that starts out from humanity as it is, and then launches toward some ideal, leaves death behind. But death is faster than we are and sooner or later it catches up with us: the father holds his dead son in his hands.

We find the key to interpretation of this scene in the Gospel. At Nain, Christ meets the funeral procession of a dead person, the only child of a widowed mother (cf. Lk 7:11-17): such is the situation of humanity. The question is life. Christ encounters humanity in its true reality. He will be the one who takes upon himself the destiny of this life oriented to death, offering us his own life in return, that is, the life of the Son who, even though he dies, is raised up by the Father. Only by opening ourselves to the gift of a life of a different quality can the human self acquire the existential certainty of the relationship that makes us capable of distinguishing our authentic individuality from our selfishness, freeing it from fear for ourselves and the instinct of wanting to subjugate everything to our needs.[3] Otherwise, if we want to take the movement of life on ourselves, not only can we not transmit it, but we can only transform it into its opposite.

---

3 Cf. V SOLOVIEV, *The Meaning of Love*. Reprinted 1985 by Lindisfarne Books, though the text here is taken from the Italian translation, *Il significato dell'amore*, (or. Russian, Moscow 1892-94) in ID., *Il significato dell'amore e altri scritti*, La Casa di Matriona, Milan 1983, 93.

Chapter 3
ABRAHAM (ABRAM):
FROM THE INDIVIDUAL TO THE PERSON

1. God calls us to a relational existence

To tackle the first dimension considered by spiritual theology, the human being as such who is marked by the tragedy of sin, we can be assisted with some episodes from Abraham's life as narrated in Genesis:

> Now the Lord said to Abram, "Go from your country and your kindred and your father's house to the land that I will show you. I will make of you a great nation, and I will bless you, and make your name great, so that you will be a blessing. I will bless those who bless you, and the one who curses you I will curse; and in you all the families of the earth shall be blessed" (Gen 12:1-3).

Abraham's story (Abram, until he begins to be called Abraham in Chapter 17) begins with a call. God makes himself heard. The God who addresses Abram is a God very close to human beings – he speaks within them. He is a God of the heart. In order for God to begin to speak to Abram, Abram does not have to do anything typically religious: he does not carve a statue, does not celebrate a particular rite, but in his heart he hears a voice, follows an intuition which comes from within that he had never before grasped.

Something absolutely new, not usual, is awakening in his heart. It is not pressure. It does not weigh him down. Abram begins to grasp an intuition, to linger on it, evaluate it, think about it, to observe it, until, slowly, this voice becomes more explicit. Abram perceives that the voice is within, but that it belongs to another, it is not his. It is not self-suggestion, in short. There must be someone who is speaking to him. Abram experiences being addressed by a word, but a word he grasps from within, in his heart.

It is a voice, an intuition, which, however, begins to orientate itself gradually, because as he acknowledges this voice and becomes familiar with it, it strengthens his awareness that there must be someone who is speaking to him. In Abram we are observing the awakening of what we can call 'relationship' – the relationship that has its source outside of him and that chooses him as its partner, as the 'you' to whom it refers. The word is more and more familiar, it is of the heart, and Abram manages to decipher it.

The relationship is so attentive, so thoughtful, that the One who speaks to him addresses Abram in Abram's way, according to his cultural and linguistic perspective, so that Abram can decipher what is awakening within him. The reader is immediately told that it is God, the Lord, who is addressing Abram. But Abram is discovering this gradually. What he does grasp is that the Other – the one who is already the Lord for the reader – is telling him to leave his land, his country, his kindred (cf. Gen 12:1).

He is told to leave his home, called 'your father's house', and to set off for a country that his mysterious interlocutor will indicate. The Word takes him out of his country and from his father's house, urges him to leave, to leave it all behind, to walk toward a place that will be shown to him.

It is clear to Abram what he is leaving; he knows it very well. But where the mysterious voice is directing him to is unknown to him. This movement, which involves the abandonment of the current situation, of relationships and of known places, guides him not toward a place – because Abram does not know where this is – but toward the one who is calling him. Abram is increasingly aware that a mutual relationship is being established between him and God: God who calls, Abram who receives the call; Abram who leaves what he has and what he knows and God who knows where he will take him, but who has not yet told this to Abram. In this way Abram learns to relate. Slowly he will grasp that if he wants to walk on he will have to speak with the Lord, because the Lord knows where to take him. The Lord holds the secret that will only slowly be revealed to Abram.

Abram will go on like this, moving away from what he has left behind and increasingly entering the 'new' which is known only to the One who calls him. This means that this 'new' must be something typical for the caller. In this way Abram will enter into a relational existence where the centre of the relationship is the other, not his own ego. Now, a natural life can also reach a certain relational consciousness, but it will always be a relationship according to nature in which the ego, as an expression of that nature, nevertheless remains the epicentre of the relationship. And relationships according to nature cannot live in relational freedom, since nature is governed by laws that express what it needs. Therefore, the Lord's call asks Abram to enter into a new way of relating, abandoning the way according to nature, that is, ties to his homeland and blood ties.

God then concludes by telling Abram that all the families of the earth will be blessed in him, that is, Abram's destiny, by leaving one family, will intertwine with families of the whole earth. Indeed, for all these families, he will become a reason for life, that is, blessing. It is no coincidence that God told him that he would make his name great (cf. Gen 12:2). In Genesis 11 the exact opposite behaviour is described: men who act alone, make their own decision, begin building a city and a tower, to 'make a name' for themselves (cf. Gen 11:4) and to reach heaven, the dwelling place of God. Instead, Abram is here to be called, it is he who is chosen by the Other and it is the Other who will make his name great. It is the Other who will show him the place. The text adds a very simple passage expressing Abram's obedience, his taking the Other seriously, whom he initially recognized only as his own voice:

> Now the Lord said to Abram, "Go from your country and your kindred and your father's house to the land that I will show you. I will make of you a great nation, and I will bless you, and make your name great, so that you will be a blessing. I will bless those who bless you, and the

one who curses you I will curse; and in you all the families of the earth shall be blessed."

So Abram went, as the Lord had told him; and Lot went with him. Abram was seventy-five years old when he departed from Haran. Abram took his wife Sarai and his brother's son Lot, and all the possessions that they had gathered, and the persons whom they had acquired in Haran; and they set forth to go to the land of Canaan. When they had come to the land of Canaan, Abram passed through the land to the place at Shechem, to the oak[a] of Moreh. At that time the Canaanites were in the land. Then the Lord appeared to Abram, and said, "To your offspring I will give this land." So he built there an altar to the Lord, who had appeared to him. 8 From there he moved on to the hill country on the east of Bethel, and pitched his tent, with Bethel on the west and Ai on the east; and there he built an altar to the Lord and invoked the name of the Lord. And Abram journeyed on by stages toward the Negeb.

Now there was a famine in the land. So Abram went down to Egypt to reside there as an alien, for the famine was severe in the land (Gen 12:4-10).

At the beginning God tells Abram to go to the land 'that I will show you.' But since he is now in this land, as soon as

Abram has arrived with his nephew a famine breaks out and Abram has to leave again. Here we can see that the 'land' is not just a place, a territory, but must necessarily have multi-layered meanings. The Lord who made himself felt in his heart wants to bring Abram to a different level of existence. This journey is not just a journey to a piece of land, but a way to a new existence. And in fact, on the road to Egypt, we will find Abram engaged in an interior struggle, with strange, even dramatic implications, but which will reveal how the path that he is called to travel concerns the way he is to exist.

2. Abram still as the individual

> When he was about to enter Egypt, he said to his wife Sarai, "I know well that you are a woman beautiful in appearance; and when the Egyptians see you, they will say, 'This is his wife'; then they will kill me, but they will let you live. Say you are my sister, so that it may go well with me because of you, and that my life may be spared on your account." When Abram entered Egypt the Egyptians saw that the woman was very beautiful. When the officials of Pharaoh saw her, they praised her to Pharaoh. And the woman was taken into Pharaoh's house. And for her sake he dealt well with Abram; and he had sheep, oxen, male donkeys, male and female slaves, female donkeys, and camels (Gen 12:11-16).

This passage brings us back to the beginning of Genesis, to the creation of Adam and Eve. Abram has a wife, but he would like her to become his sister, to renounce being a wife, that is, to change her identity. But if she became his sister, they (she and Abram) would be children of the same father. Not only does Abram want Sarai (she only becomes Sarah in Chapter 17) to become his sister, but even a kind of mother, since what Abram asks of Sarai is protection, like a child asking his mother to defend him because he fears for himself. Because of the fear he feels for himself, Abram prefers to even be a kind of child, immature, and therefore would like to deny his husband's bond with Sarai.

In this passage there is a sort of return to Genesis 2:18, where the woman (*isha*) is taken by the man (*ish*), that is to say, they are different. This 'split' into the masculine and feminine which we find at the beginning of human nature, is not yet altogether different, since it is qualified by the expression 'flesh of my flesh' (cf. Gen 2:23). Only in the next verse, when it is said that the man will leave his father, his mother and his house to join himself with her, does the woman begin to be a real other. At first she is similar to man, then she becomes his other. And it is only with real otherness that unity can be experienced. They leave as similar, leave their home to join with the other. And only in this unity with an other is there true relationship. Abram, on the other hand, would like to deny the reality of his relationship with Sarai – that of husband and wife – and thus reveals the truth of the fact that he has not yet discovered someone other than himself in Sarai. We are in a situation similar to Genesis 11:1, when 'the whole earth had one language and the same words,' where differences did not exist, and where the difference necessary for a real going out of oneself was perceived as a threat, a source of fear, division. The other, meaning Sarai, represents not only a serious limitation for Abram, but a real threat. This is why Abram wants to deny her her identity.

With this, the reason for infertility is unveiled to the reader: there is no unity of a love that includes the one who is different, who creates his or her unity with a real other, but it is a relationship still linked to their same human nature. For this reason Abram prefers Sarai the sister to Sarai the wife. But Abram had been invited by God to leave his homeland and his father's house, two realities belonging to the order of nature. The family, and then family extended to include the people of a territory – that is, his homeland – are categories of the natural order, as Bulgakov clearly explains,[1] therefore marked by necessity, where gender always runs the risk of diluting the person and where the bond of love and sacrifice for the other is often self-love disguised under collective appearances. Now Abram shows that a relationship founded on the needs of nature does not withstand the threat to its existence. Abram, frightened for himself, sees in Sarai and her beauty the reason that pushes him to deny his wife's identity and, consequently, his own. He would like to return to the nest where his self can hide in nature. He would like to submerge his self and Sarai's in a primary bond of nature.

---

1 Cf. S Bulgakov, *Nacija i čelovečestvo [Nation and humanity]*, in *Novyj Grad [Città Nuova]* 8 (1934), 28-38. By the same author, cf. also *Razmyšlenija o nacional'nosti [Thoughts on nationality]*, in Id., *Dva grada [The two cities]*, Put', Moscow 1911, 278-303.

In this view of things, even what is most characteristic of Sarai, her beauty, becomes an attribute of her nature – it does not belong to Sarai in relational terms. Thus another person who has no relationship with Sarai can enjoy it. This is a profound issue because in this story one understands that there is a way of living one's nature which is not only according to nature, but where nature belongs to a face, has a name. Abram, paralyzed by fear for himself, would like the name to be erased, the face to disappear and only the beauty of nature to emerge. If it appears that this beauty belongs to a name that is made up of a relationship – that is, to her as a wife and therefore involving him as a husband – another who would like to take possession of this beauty would have to kill him to join with Sarai. The episode is therefore extremely important from a spiritual point of view: God is calling Abram to an *exodus* from life as an 'individual', inasmuch as the individual is the expression of his own nature. The voice of the Lord calls Abram to leave this individual existence submerged in nature and enter into a new existence, where the foundation of everything is relationship, a personal existence. The basis of human existence is not human nature, but what the Greek Fathers called *hypostasis* – that which underlies everything – that is, the person.[2] It is an existence not 'according to one's own species' (cf. Gen 1:11;12:25), but according to God. Hence

2 "Man is transcendent to the world and, in this sense, is free from the world, is non-world. He is not exhausted by any *quid*, no definition circumscribes him, but he is, like God, an absolute *non-quid*. He places all worldly affairs outside and before him, like a certain *quid*, remaining free and transcendent before

the mystery of the call is protected by God, so that Abram may learn to choose the Other first and to stop navel-gazing, to look elsewhere than attachment to his natural existence to orient himself to be open to and acknowledge the other.

3. *God is person, his existence is communal*

At this point, it is convenient to interrupt the path of Abram's initiation into the covenant for a moment and call our attention to God's way of existing because God is calling Abram to this, and it is according to this manner of existence that the redeemed human being, in Christ, will be constituted. True spiritual life, therefore, is humanity lived according to this manner of existence.

The Greek Fathers spent three whole centuries telling their fellow countrymen what the novelty that Christ brought to the world consists of. In fact, they soon became aware that the intellectual structure of classical thinking could not be used to explain the novelty that humanity had received from Christ. Greek thinking believed that the reality at the basis of existence is being, and with being, the nature of things and the search for the ideal essence of things.

---

it. Even more so, man transcends himself in all his empirical or psychological data, in every self-determination that leaves the calm of his absolute inviolate and his depth undisturbed": S BULGAKOV, *Unfading Light*. Grand Rapids, MI: Wm. B. Eerdmans Publish. Co., though the text here is taken from the Italian translation, *La luce senza tramonto*, (or. Russian, Moscow 1917) Lipa, Rome 2002, 319.

The experience of the Fathers was that Christ had brought Christians a radical change of life. But for Greek thinking, life was much less than being. The Fathers, then, with the key to life, could not enter into the foundations of existence according to classical thought. The simple observation that a stone is not alive but it does exist, has being, showed the intellectual difficulty of locating life in what was considered to be the foundation. But the experience of Christian life in the first centuries, which were centuries of witness, shows that although they were not yet able to explain Christ, they were able to manifest him, reveal him, let him be seen. The testimony of the early centuries is dramatically marked by martyrdom. And it is martyrdom, life offered up out of love, because of the relationship with God and other martyrs, that highlighted for intellectual research the fact that when we talk about life we talk about it as a relationship, gift of self, as inclusion of the other.

It is more than this. For Greek thought, God is such only if he is an absolute and unlimited being. He cannot tolerate another absolute being beside himself. Christ, on the other hand, manifests a unity of life, of will, of energy with God whom he relates to and calls Father, and who is also the source and cause of the existence of the Spirit. The Persons of the Trinity do not seem to claim any autonomy, indeed one refers to the other and it is precisely in this reference that each Person recognizes his identity.

To make themselves understood by the intellectuals of their time, the Fathers, especially the Cappadocians, reflected on God's manner of existence, that is, his way of being: God exists in a relational way. God's way of existing is communal, relational. It is not a question of how being is regarded in classical thought, nor of life understood in natural terms, but of both being and life taken up in an absolute sense according to God's existence. The Fathers thus succeeded in revealing that communion, relationship, love are found in ontology, that is, in the foundations of existence. They let go of the most common term used for person in their day, that is, *prosōpon*, a term they had also used. It was a term that had come to mean the mask worn by actors in the theatre, and which therefore alluded too strongly to the illusory aspect of the individual, while also saying how, through this mask, the human being acquires some taste of the freedom denied him by the logical and moral laws of the world in which he lives.[3] The Fathers preferred a philosophical term to this one, one that did not in itself mean person in their time, but because it was not tied to other specific meanings for people its meaning could be shaped: *hypostasis* (*sub-sistentia*, what lies beneath). Underneath, in the foundations of existence, there lies a personal existence. Therefore, person means an entity defined by relationship. The person emerges from relationships, as, for example, the noun 'husband' is not an autonomous term, but also implies the existence of a wife. If there is no wife, there is no husband. Likewise, the Fathers say: beneath existence there is the person, that is, a personal,

---

3 Cf. I Zizioulas, B*eing as Communion. Studies in Personhood and the Church* (Crestwood, NY: St Vladimir's Seminary Press, 1997), though the text here is taken from the Italian translation, *L'essere ecclesiale*, (or. Fr., Geneva 1981) Qiqajon, Magnano 2007, 29.

relational identity of God. So God's way of existing is that of the Father, because when I say 'Father', I am talking of the personal origin, the movement towards the generation of the other, I am talking about the originating relationship that also includes the other, who is the Son.[4] And when I say 'Son', I am talking about a relational, communal existence, because the other is included, that is, the Father.[5] But the difficult thing for a simply natural understanding was to

4 "For what mutual relation is so closely and concordantly engrafted and fitted together as that meaning of relation to the Father expressed by the word Son? And a proof of this is that even if both of these names be not spoken, that which is omitted is connoted by the one that is uttered, so closely is the one implied in the other, and concordant with it: and both of them are so discerned in the one that one cannot be conceived without the other": GREORY OF NYSSA, *Contra Eumonius*, IV, 8 (*PG* 45, 669C but available online in English, e.g. http://www.newadvent.org/fathers/290104.htm); "When mention is made of the Father, who is in the Son. If the Son is named, the Father is in the Son, and the Spirit is not outside the Word": ATHANSIUS OF ALEXANDRIA, *Letters to Serapion* 1,14 (PG 26, 565A) but also in English as 'The Letters Of Saint Athanasius Concerning The Holy Spirit to Bishop Serapion', From the translation with introduction and notes by C.R.B. Shapland, originally published Epworth Press, 1951.

5 "Then again God is called 'Son' ... because he is the living image of his Sire ... in the Son the mystery of the divine Father is made manifest: Face that confronts God's own as in a mirror ... Two countenances then in one God. Two persons, distinct in all reality and truth ... Between them exists something unknown to man that makes possible their existence as two separate Beings yet with one life, one essence unhampered by the limitations of self which protect and isolate all other life. Between Creator and Creator everything is open; the closed doors of individuality are non-existent. The given condition, likewise unknown to man, that makes this possible is of course perfection of person ... All this means that God is 'Spirit' ... It is in him, the Third Person

think of this relationship itself as being a personal existence, that is, the Holy Spirit, whom the Fathers called the love of God's love, the *vinculum* or bond of love that unites the Father and the Son.[6]

4. *An existence that includes otherness*

With this great novelty, the Fathers gave a decisive contribution to the resolution of what for Greek thought was an insurmountable difficulty: otherness, relationship as a true realization of being rather than a lessening of it. The idea of being existing as a relationship was foreign to the intellectual perspective of ancient thought. Hence, when the Fathers spoke about the unity of God's being as *communion*, in terms different from those of substance, they also gave an intellectual contribution to reflection on the truth of

---

of the Trinity, that Father and Son are powerfully individual, yet one. R GUARDINI *The Lord*, Gateway editions (from original 1954 Regnery Publishing), 2016 Impression, 506-507.

6 Cf. Augustine, *De Trinitate*, 8,10, 14 in *Opere di Sant'Agostino*, IV, Città Nuova, Rome 1987, 359 or see *The Trinity, Works of St. Augustine*, ed. John Rotelle, New City Press, 2016. Richard of St Victor, developing the idea that love is not a closed circle, and that to be perfect there is need not only of mutuality, but also sharing, states: "The communication of love cannot happen at all if amongst less than three persons ... on the other hand we rightly speak of co-love when a third person is loved by the two, in harmony and with a communal spirit. We rightly speak of co-love when the two persons' affects are fused so as to become only one because of the flame of love for the third" *Richard of St Victor On the Trinity* English Translation and Commentary, Ruben Angelici, Cascade Books 2011,127-128. Cf also S. BULGAKOV, *Ipostas' i ipostasnost'[Ipostasi e ipostaticità]*, in *Sbornik statej posvjaščennych Petru Berngardoviču Struve [Collection of articles by P.B. Struve]*, Praha 1925, 356-357.

existence.[7] In concrete terms, this means that the many are not a limit or threat to the one, and that the one is not pitted against or inclined to incorporate and manage the many, but that it is precisely the communal existence which brings about the one and the many. Unity and otherness emerge from relationships. Therefore a totally different scenario opens up for relationships between people, between groups, between peoples, precisely because in Christ, God made himself known as Father. The tri-unitarian vision of God and the manifestation of the communion of the three persons reveal one only God who lives in the manner of persons. Unity is not due to the unity of nature, but is the expression of communion, it is the affirmation of communion. This is why unity is free and not subjected to the needs of the laws and logic that every nature brings with it.

From this we can see that the relational existence typical of the person is expressed in the nature that the Three share: the Father stamps the imprint of fatherhood on divine nature, meaning he generates. The Son impresses his way of being as a generated being on all the divine nature which he too possesses, and therefore he expresses it in filial and obedient love to the Father. And the Holy Spirit impresses his way of being on divine nature, his 'spiration' (breath) which is the life of the Father and of the Son, communion.

---

7 "the three have one Nature — God. And the union is the Father from Whom and to Whom the order of Persons runs its course, not so as to be confounded, but so as to be possessed, without distinction of time, of will, or of power.": GREGORY OF NAZIANZEN, *Oration 42, The Last Farewell*, 15. English translation taken from http://www.newadvent.org/fathers/310242.htm.

He is the Lord of communion. God therefore exists in such a way as to give a wholly personal and relational existence to all of divine nature, in an integral and total way.

In becoming incarnate, Christ also gives the imprint of his personal or filial existence to the human nature he has assumed. The Incarnation represents a sort of exorcism against the dark countenance of nature. The taking on of flesh by the Son of God means that the person awakens in the human being, lives and develops in an inseparable unity of spiritual and psycho-somatic experience, so that his or her spirit lives psychosomatically – bodiliness and psyche are conditioned by the spirit. It is precisely in Christ that the Father created and redeemed humanity, because only in the Son can human nature be lived in a relational, communal, filial way.[8]

5. *God communicates his 'tropos' to human beings*

God has shaped humanity in his image and likeness. He created us so that we might live our humanity in a communal, relational way, the way of love.[9] Even though human nature

---

8 "We are all in fact in Christ, and the common person of humanity rediscovers life in him ... The Word dwelt amongst us by means of only person only [Christ] so that, as the true and only Son of God, his dignity might pass into all of humanity according to the Spirit of holiness, and so that by means of one person only these words might be fulfilled: I say: you are gods, children of the Most High, all of you (Ps 82:6; Jn 10:34": ATHANASIUS OF ALEXANDRIA, taken from *L'incarnazione del Verbo di Dio e contro gli ariani*, 8 (PG 26, 996C).

9 "What the Son of God is by nature in his Incarnation (and it is clear that he is holy and without sin), they have also done by grace: he calls Christ's way of living the Image of God":

is created, is given, and human freedom cannot constitute it, it has nevertheless been given the possibility of existing as a personal *hypostasis*, as is the case with God. God does not communicate what he is (his nature), because the abyss between the created and uncreated cannot be bridged, but he gives us the gift of *how* he lives (that is, his *tropos*, or 'way of being', his *hypostasis*).[10] The Son of God overcomes the abyss of natures by adapting his own *tropos*, that is, his way of existing in divine life, to human nature. And even created existence undergoes changes in this union, not changes to its nature, but to its *tropos*, its manner of existence, whereby it experiences human nature in the manner of God.[11]

This awareness of existing in and for relationship as a person is precisely the communal self. After sin – which is precisely the fall from an existence where life is realized on the level of the person existing as a natural individual seeking to achieve survival from within and from his or her own efforts – an element of this still remains in our self-awareness, only now it is no longer communal, but individual. This self then becomes the expression of its very

---

николемус the Hagiorite, *Nicodemus of the Holy Mountain: A Handbook of Spiritual Counsel* (Classics of Western Spirituality). Mahwah, NJ: Paulist Press, 1988, though the text is taken from the Italian translation, *Manuale di consigli ovvero sulla tutela dei cinque sensi*, Ed. S. Schoinas, Volos, 1969, 210.

10 This distinction goes back to the Cappadocian Fathers, but it was Maximus the Confessor who made it a key concept in theology. Cf. *Ambigua I,* (*PG* 91, 1036C); 67 (*PG* 91, 1400s); 5 (*PG* 91, 1053B), etc.

11 Therefore St John Damascene can speak of the Incarnation as "a second way of existing" of the Logos (*C. Jacob.* 52: *PG* 94, 1464A).

nature, subject to the limits of its own created existence and enslaved to its needs. If God exists in such a way that each divine person expresses himself in his divine nature, after sin the human being becomes an expression of his nature.

The fear of death is certainly the most immediate characteristic of an individual self that finds the foundation of its existence in its nature, since this nature is fragmented into many individuals in conflict, is wounded and consigned to death. The self as an expression of nature, but at the same time as self-consciousness, lives in the tension between the threat of death looming over it – hence the threat of its disappearance – and the spasmodic desire to save itself, which it believes is bound up with overcoming the limits of individuality, therefore something universal, where another is present. But at the same time this universal where the other is objectively present also represents a threat to the self. The presence of the other is indeed a risk, but at the same time we need the other. In this situation, our 'communion' is a compromise built on the defences that protect us from the implicit danger that the other represents for us. Hence the desire to annihilate the other and eliminate its difference. Genesis 11:1 expresses the human attempt to bring everything back to the one, and Genesis 12:11-13 tells of Abram who wants to smother Sarai's personal identity as Sarai (his wife) by hiding her in kinship (his sister), that is, in nature. But God promised Abram that 'in you all the families of the earth shall be blessed' (Gen 12:3), that is, there will be an abundance of life in families and peoples because of Abram. A solution is then proposed that maintains diversity, which extends to universality and which is rooted precisely in Abram as a person.

We have already stressed that the mystery of this new existence, of this new 'land' God wants to bring Abram to, is in the hands of the Lord, who precisely for this reason will be discovered as the One who is present between Abram and Sarai, allowing them to experience communion in otherness. Until their true relationship as husband and wife exists between them, life will not emerge. The true unity between man and woman is not due to their kindred relationship as brother and sister, which is of the order of nature, and belongs to the country that Abram was invited to leave behind. And it is not a union that is an expression of the natural instinct between male and female, but the becoming 'one flesh' (see Gen 2:24), that is, a single human situation, thanks to a freely chosen unity, to the fulfilment of love, and not to an instinct of nature. It is only freely chosen unity that becomes unshakeable communion. So, the relationship that Abram now begins to have with God, where the other comes first, becomes paradigmatic of what must happen between him and Sarai: Sarai must come first for him, not in a possessive way, but in the way that Abram is learning by growing in his relationship with God. Until this happens there will not be life for them, because their fruitfulness will depend on the way both of them live out their being husband and wife, their identity. One cannot arrive at true fatherhood and motherhood – not according to nature, but in a personal way – except through a free relationship, a love that unites freely, which makes room for God.

God therefore has a vision of Abram as a father, and for this he must bring him to the truth of his union with Sarai, which he will only arrive at through his relationship with the Lord. It is therefore the relationship with God that will become the foundation of the relationship with Sarai. So much so that there is no unity at the moment. There is a unity of instinct, which crumbles when a stronger instinct takes over. Then *erōs* gives in to *thanatos*. Brother and sister are no longer categories that can save Abram. He is called to find his wife, but to find her in God.

After completing creation, culminating in the creation of man, as the mosaic presents it so masterfully in the Cathedral at Monreale, God finds himself alone within creation, because all things live 'according to their species' (see Gen 1:11-12:21), that is, according to their nature. Only God is not 'according to nature', but 'according to the relationship between persons' (fig. 3).

Therefore God creates the human being 'according to his image',[12] to talk to himself, to have a relationship, so that man is a sort of 'you', an interlocutor of God's in creation. Of all creation, the only 'you' of God is humanity (fig. 4).

---

12 Among the Fathers it is above all Athanasius who develops a doctrine of the image according to which the image proper does not have to be attributed to human beings, but the *kat 'eikona*, "according to the image": the human being does not possess the property of image, but shares in the image, which is the eternal Son. Therefore, through Christ, the Incarnate Word, human beings share in the intimate relations of the divine Persons. Cf. R. BERNARD, *L'image de Dieu d'après saint Athanase*, Au-bier, Paris 1952, 32-42.

But God sees that it is not good for the man to be alone. Then he creates Eve, who at the beginning is presented as a kind of 'splitting' of the human being into male and female (fig. 5).

But in the following image depicted in the mosaics, God leads Eve to Adam (see Gen 2:22), to underline that it is He who creates and guarantees the relationship of these two 'others', no longer according to their species – that is, not according to nature, like the rest of creation – but according to the typical existence of God himself, that is according to a way of being relational – the person as existence constituted by relationship with the other (fig. 6).

Through his presence, with the communion that is his life, God inspires a communal existence in the human being. God takes Eve by the wrist and, with his left hand, moves it toward Adam's wrist. The pulse is the place where life is measured, where its beat is noted. And the life that he gives to Adam and Eve is according to the existence of God, that is, a relational life where the relationship is the Lord.

In the Genesis 12:10-20 episode, God has led Abram to admit that he is still a solitary man who has not yet discovered the God who unites him and Sarai. So immediately, without too much regret, to save himself he sacrifices Sarai. It is Abram's first sacrifice, quite a different one, as we shall see, from the sacrifice of his son. But this time he does it because he is attached to himself, because he sees only himself, because he is an individual and tries to save himself by sacrificing the other, fully consistent with the saying, *mors tua vita mea.*

Being still the individual, therefore in the state to which sin has reduced the human being, Abram acts as the one who is the master of good and evil. Sin has convinced human beings that they will have great personal advantage if they are the ones to manage the knowledge of good and evil. And here we see how this management works from a practical point of view. Sarai's beauty is good in itself, but now this beauty represents a threat for Abram, the risk of something evil, even though Abram had enjoyed it up till now.

Which means that Abram does not have an objective concept of good and evil, but he is the arbiter, and he wants good for himself. By excluding the other, this good is no longer good for the other. Since the good of the other – Sarai's beauty – is a threat to him, Abram acts in a way that makes this good bad for the other – meaning he abandons Sarai – in order to save what is good for himself. What the Egyptians could do to him because of Sarai's beauty becomes the persuasive factor that convinces him to turn good into bad to save himself. So it is not simply a question of the fact that he desires evil for the other and good for himself, but that he converts what is the other's good into what is bad for her.

God reverses the situation through Pharaoh, and unmasks Abram's selfish interpretation of good and evil. Only when Abram enters into communion will he discover the truth as an objective reality. Only when he experiences a relationship with God will he discover Sarai as a wife, and become a father. He will then enter into fatherhood not according to nature, but according to the Spirit – whom

God wants to lead him to. Therefore, the true 'country' towards which Abram is walking is fatherhood according to the order of the Spirit, something St Paul would later evoke: every fatherhood takes its name, has its origin, its foundation, its source in heavenly fatherhood (cf. Eph 3:14-15).

It is to this end that God brings Abram out of his father's house, so that he may begin to free himself from a fatherhood according to nature and enter on a path that will lead him to a life according to the Spirit of God, that is, according to a father-son way of living, a life of union among persons.

Here we grasp the meaning of Chapter 15, where God concludes a covenant with Abram in which he engages in a unilateral covenant sealed with a sworn oath of imprecation. Abram has to cut the animals in two and wait for the covenant to be sealed in the deep of night by a fire that passes through their torn bodies. The very form of the rite makes the seriousness of the covenant visible: if one of the two parties does not keep it, then what happened to the animals will happen to him. At the same time, especially seen from a Syriac patristic background where fire is a frequent symbol of the Spirit and of divine life, the scene can also be read as the return of the Spirit to this human situation which, without this breath, dominates all of creation. The covenant is a further step by which God takes Abram out of nature, separates him from the rest of the animal creation, to promote him to an existence of fire, spirit, a life according to God. The relationship with God becomes the pivot around which Abram's identity turns. Abram had heard: *'I will make your name great ... This man shall not be your heir; no one but your very own issue shall be your heir'* (Gen 12:2; cf. Gen 15:3-4). The Lord himself had brought him out into the night and told him: *'Look toward heaven and count the stars, if you are able to count them,'* and then adds: *'So shall your descendants be'* (cf. Gen15:5). But Abram does not yet have a son. On the one hand, his faith in the One who speaks to him is firm, and he also receives confirmation, because this God leads him to interpret his story, making him grasp how he has intervened: *'I am the Lord who brought you from Ur of the Chaldeans, to give you this land to possess'* (Gen 15:7). And he also makes it clear that there is an additional meaning to these interventions.

Abram begins to see that country, or land as territory, was the literal meaning, the first layer of this call, but that the One who speaks to him wants to lead him to something else. Little by little, he begins to realize that this is a different quality of life, one he cannot even imagine at this stage. So his desire remains fixed on descendants, on the heir, on giving birth to a son, which is something he knows how to do. So, in Chapter 16, he generates a son with Hagar, Sarai's slave.

6. The beginning of the spiritual life is acceptance, welcome

> When Abram was ninety-nine years old, the Lord appeared to Abram, and said to him, "I am God Almighty; walk before me, and be blameless. And I will make my covenant

between me and you, and will make you exceedingly numerous." Then Abram fell on his face; and God said to him, "As for me, this is my covenant with you: You shall be the ancestor of a multitude of nations. No longer shall your name be Abram, but your name shall be Abraham; for I have made you the ancestor of a multitude of nations. I will make you exceedingly fruitful; and I will make nations of you, and kings shall come from you (Gen 17:1-6).

We are in the chapter which introduces circumcision, where Abraham again hears the promise concerning his fatherhood. But he is invited to understand that he is not the one who is to worry about becoming a father. The son generated with Hagar was once again his attempt to circumvent the promise, again not respecting the identity of husband and wife and entering into a compromise with nature whereby, if he is to have a descendant, then a slave will do equally as well. Paul would say that whoever unites with a prostitute becomes one with her (cf. 1 Cor 6:16). Whoever unites with a slave begins to take the path of slavery, that is, to once more submerge self-awareness in the needs of nature and be enslaved by such needs. Through a pedagogy of covenant in which he learns to live the truth of relationships, that is, where the other comes first, Abraham begins to sense that the promise of life linked to the gift of fatherhood will not be fulfilled according to the needs of a natural relationship. Rather does God want to carry out through him the plan described in the creation of Adam and Eve: God is the 'third' partner there, whose presence –

which is life and communion – in freely given love can join a man and a woman and give them real fertility, since not only biological life is given, life according to nature, according to one's species, but life according to the Holy Spirit, who is the Lord who gives love (cf. Rom 5:5).

Precisely because the relationship between husband and wife is the relationship *par excellence*, two people who love one another encounter one another in such a way that at the same time a third person, the God of love, is with them: *While the third is present / And that third is love.*[13]

> The Lord appeared to Abraham by the oaks of Mamre, as he sat at the entrance of his tent in the heat of the day. He looked up and saw three men standing near him. When he saw them, he ran from the tent entrance to meet them, and bowed down to the ground. He said, "My lord, if I find favour with you, do not pass by your servant. Let a little water be brought, and wash your feet, and rest yourselves under the tree" (Gen 18:1-4).

Abraham and Sarah (they are now renamed after Chapter 17) are alone and elderly, at noon. She will be inside the tent, Abraham outside, probably dozing in the heat. Now, having reached old age, Abraham's attention is directed to the Other. He still hopes that what he was told by the One who had called him to leave his homeland, his father's house, will be fulfilled.

---

13 V Ivanov, *Mysli o simvolizme [Thoughts on symbolism]*, in *Sobr. Soč.*, II, Žizn's Bogom, Brussels 1974, 606.

fig. 1 *Laocoon and His Sons*, Vatican Museums

fig. 2 *The Raft of the Medusa*, Jean Louis Théodore Géricault, Paris, Louvre

fig. 3 *God rests on the seventh day*, The cycle of creation, Archdiocese of Monreale, Basilica and Cathedral of Santa Maria Nuova

fig. 4 *Man and beasts are created on the sixth day*, The cycle of creation, Archdiocese of Monreale, Basilica and Cathedral of Santa Maria Nuova

fig. 5 *The creation of woman*, Man and woman in Paradise, Archdiocese of Monreale, Basilica and Cathedral of Santa Maria Nuova

fig. 6 *God introduces woman to Adam*, Man and woman in Paradise, Archdiocese of Monreale, Basilica and Cathedral of Santa Maria Nuova

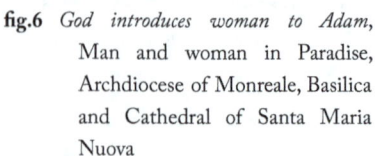

fig.7 Baptismal font, North Church, Shivta, Israel

fig.8 Baptsimal font in the Church known as San Vitale in Sbeitla, the ancient Sufetula, Tunisia

fig.9 Basilica of St Mary Magdalene, Vézelay Abbey: spots of sun in the centre of the main leading to the altar only during the summer solstice

fig.10 Basilica of St Mary Magdalene, Vézelay Abbey: sunlit illumination of the capitals during the winter solstice

At a certain moment '*he looked up*' (v. 2). Both in the Old and the New Testaments it is a gesture of openness towards the encounter with the Lord or with one of his messengers, at least to see the place where the encounter will take place. The author of these words thus already creates the atmosphere of a meeting of great importance. The gesture of looking up and seeing the guests immediately announces a visit that comes from above, promises an intervention from God.

Abraham sees three men in front of him. Without delay, even though he is now an old man, he starts running to welcome them. Undoubtedly he saw something of importance in them as soon as he saw them, because he prostrates himself on the ground. In the Samaritan Pentateuch, which according to many experts is older than the official Hebrew text, Abraham addresses the three. They are three, while Abraham and Sarah are two. Two is not yet communion according to God. It is not yet a fruitful relationship, while the three guests who present themselves before Abraham represent completeness in this numerical sense.[14] Abraham has already taken on so much of the covenant mentality, that he focuses his attention on the

---

14 "The monad is set in motion by virtue of its richness; the dyad is superseded, because divinity is above matter and form; the triad is defined for its perfection, since it is the first that overcomes the composition of the dyad. Thus divinity does not remain limited nor does it expand indefinitely. The former would be without honour, the latter contrary to order; the former would be purely Jewish, the latter Hellenic and polytheistic": GREGORY OF NAZIANZEN, *Orazione XXIII*, 8 (PG 33, 1160CD). Note: while select orations of Gregory are available in English, no. 23 does not appear to be readily available either in print or online.

other and immediately says that it would be good for them not to go on, but to stop, considering they are travellers and the heat of the noonday sun.

According to custom, he will have water brought to wash their feet and therefore invites them to sit under the tree. Abraham gives great attention to the three guests and begins a welcoming ritual that is carefully described, emphasizing the hurried movements which are so much a contrast to his old age, so as to highlight how hospitality and welcome release energy, strength and rapid gestures in Abraham that he would not normally have due to his age.

Here is the first sign of how hospitality, welcome, begins to transfigure human nature. Something is being grafted onto nature that makes it live another way: the three, letting themselves be welcomed, immediately energize Abraham. This is the relationship Abraham has entered into by taking the covenant journey, which brought him to an acceptance that involves his whole person, including his relationships, his wife included.

Here we need to be very careful, because in our culture, welcome and acceptance are normally considered something passive. For the ancients, instead, it was an investment of energies, strengths, an integral activity, an effort that requires the whole person to be involved. And it is precisely for this reason that the person begins to change his or her life. It is precisely acceptance that transforms it.

The guests accept all the attention and tell Abraham: '*Do as you have said*' (Gen 18:5). The writer continues the account closely: '*And Abraham hastened into the tent to Sarah, and said,*

"*Make ready quickly three measures of choice flour, knead it, and make cakes.*"' (v. 6). Sarah too becomes involved in the hasty preparations, which she has to do 'quickly', while Abraham ran to the herd: '*took a calf, tender and good, and gave it to the servant, who hastened to prepare it*' (v. 7).

7. *The greatness of the gift depends on the welcome shown*

Abraham prepares the meal with surprising speed and then serves it to the three guests, remaining standing while they eat. Even the quantity of prepared food is exaggerated: for three people he has cooked a calf and bread made from what is equivalent to at least 35 litres of flour!

All this abundance is to stress that hospitality, welcome, releases a doting love, love that exaggerates. As a counter-image of this kind of welcome we have episodes in the Gospels where instead of enjoying exaggerated hospitality there is talk of waste (see Mt 26:8, Mk 14:4). The Letter to the Hebrews comments on the generous and zealous welcome Abraham showed his guests in the following words: 'Do not neglect to show hospitality to strangers, for by doing that some have entertained angels without knowing it' (Heb13:2).

Abraham gradually grasps the true identity of the messengers, and discovers it through the words addressed to him about his lineage:

> They said to him, "Where is your wife Sarah?" And he said, "There, in the tent." Then one said, "I will surely return to you in due season, and your wife Sarah shall have a son." And Sarah

was listening at the tent entrance behind him.
(Gen 18:9-10)

In the East, hospitality is sacred and the guest can enjoy a freedom that is truly his alone. But there is one topic that the guest never touched upon: the master's wife. Here, however, these guests not only ask for his wife but also know her name, a sign that they are involved in Abraham's story, know his difficulties, his desires, his despair, so intimately that they know of the history of his relationship with Sarah and their expectation of a child.

It is precisely in these two verses that it seems that there is a shift from the plural to the singular: from 'they said' to 'one said: "I will surely return to you,"' all in the singular. Abraham has accepted a visit from God. God's life is communal. He welcomes life as communion and, within this acceptance of life, he reveals to him the voice he was already used to hearing, the voice of the One who called him and said 'I will make you' 'I will ...', and now he tells him : 'I will return' – confirming the announcement once again.

While the guest was talking, Sarah listened as she stood at the entrance to the tent, finding herself right behind the guest who was speaking. Now the writer adds, to help the reader grasp the purpose of the event: *'Now Abraham and Sarah were old, advanced in age; it had ceased to be with Sarah after the manner of women. So Sarah laughed to herself, saying, "After I have grown old, and my husband is old, shall I have pleasure?"'* (vv. 11-12).

Sarah 'laughs to herself.' Her thinking does not go straight to childbirth but rather to conception. While

Abraham speaks all the time about lineage – and therefore of being a father – Sarah first contemplates her identity as a wife, and only later as a mother. This fact shows once again how the fruitfulness of life will depend on the right identity of the relationship between the two, and that the right relationship between the two cannot be according to nature, because otherwise it is a return to the father's house, to the homeland they left behind. God wants to detach them from the level of natural life and bring them to life according to faith, that is according to the Spirit. It is then that her identity as wife will be achieved, when their relationship includes the third person, that is, the Lord of the covenant. And since the Third is now present and they have really welcomed him with all that they are, the miracle can take place. The guest goes on to say that he heard Sarah laugh. Evidently it was not just an inner laughter, or the guest has a different perception and scrutinizes hearts!

The dialogue continues: *'The Lord said to Abraham, "Why did Sarah laugh, and say, 'Shall I indeed bear a child, now that I am old?' Is anything too wonderful for the Lord? At the set time I will return to you, in due season, and Sarah shall have a son"'* (vv. 13-14).

Sarah hears this, and because she has had a dramatic experience of her relationship with Abraham when strangers are involved, she is afraid and denies having laughed: *'"I did not laugh"; for she was afraid. He said, "Oh yes, you did laugh"'* (v. 15).

Behind this story of Sarah's laughter, the writer helps us to grasp what really happened: by welcoming the Three, welcoming communion, her inner life begins to smile: 'He laughs' is Isaac's name. In fact, Sarah will give birth to her son, who will bear the very name of the smile with which the episode of hospitality ended.

In verse 22:' *So the men turned from there, and went toward Sodom, while Abraham remained standing before the Lord* ' – Abraham now recognizes the presence of the Lord and remains before the Lord and begins to intercede on behalf of Sodom. It is a gesture that shows that Abraham begins to know the Lord in his own history, which means knowing him as the merciful Lord. This is why he begins to intercede for people in Sodom. Having received life according to God, Abraham does not reason only according to nature, but begins to reason according to his guest, according to the One who is speaking to him, according to the One who brought him out of his country and from his father's house. With this, Abraham begins openly to reveal his character as a believer. Now he can understand his call, whereas before, when he was still reasoning according to nature, it was impossible for him. In fact, he can understand his call only in relation to the Lord, in dialogue with him. Only in this relationship will the meaning of his desire to be a father begin to unfold. Had Abraham been content with having a child according to nature, he would never have been able to understand the true meaning of his call. Abraham knows he can have children because he has already had one by Hagar, but now the life he has received – that is, the Lord – tells him that Sarah will give birth. Not that he will have a child, but that Sarah will give birth. What seems impossible will now come true, to show Abraham that his fatherhood does not depend on him, because the son must come from his wife, who was obviously sterile. But, because of acceptance, of the welcome he has given, the relationship towards Sarah changes and fatherhood and motherhood must come about *'not of blood or of the will of the flesh or of the will of man, but of God'* (Jn 1:13).

They become like the one whom they have welcomed. It is not a question, then, of doing something, but of being so active in acceptance as these two elderly people, Abraham and Sarah, were, because what we welcome as communion carries within it the meaning of our existence, reveals the meaning of our vocation. Abraham accepted the Triad, communion, who prophesied what would happen. Our vocation, therefore, depends on communion. As 1 Corinthians 1:9 says, 'by him you were called into the fellowship of his Son.' Our vocation is life, life as communion, which is realized not according to our will, nor according to the laws of nature, but according to the will of God. And God's will is accepted precisely in our efforts at hospitality. The stronger our welcome, the stronger the presence. The more generous we are in making room for the guest, the greater the understanding of the message of life will be that God's will bears within. We offer our food so that we will be nourished by the new food which is the Father's will (cf. Jn 4:34).

With this visit, we have reached a significant moment in the covenant journey. The significant moment concerns the consciousness of the self, the way in which human beings perceive themselves. As we have seen with Adam and Eve (*'it is not good for the man to be alone'*, Gen 2:18), according to creation the consciousness of the self is relational, because God himself is the relationship between the two of them. Relationship is indeed part of human identity. The self is created as relational and this relationship is open to the true source of the relationship – God, who is communion. Sin has immersed our humanity in nature, but the self remains alive in its self-consciousness, only now our self-consciousness is individual, no longer relational. This individual consciousness, as we have noted, on the one hand suffers fragility, weakness and mortality typical of the natural state, but on the other, a trace, a memory of relationship remains in us, which makes us dream and want to be open to the universal.

But we do not say that this situation necessarily opens up automatically to relationship. It can also generate leanings toward idealism with which individuals console themselves and try to convince themselves that the higher the goals, the more existence will be assured. It can also happen that the relational trace left in the individual self, which aims directly at encounter with the other, becomes the impulse of *eros* in search of biological union. In fact, God has placed such a force of *eros* in human beings, a force that drives the individual to seek the other to unite with. But this union is urged and managed by a need rooted in nature itself, which therefore cannot surmount another need that causes fear – death – and therefore is generated and dies.[15]

---

15 Cf. V. Solovyev, *The Meaning of Love*, Edinburgh: Floris, 1985, though the text is taken from the Italian translation, *Il significato dell'amore,* (or. Russian, Moscow 1892-94) in Id., *Il significato dell'amore e altri scritti*, La Casa di Matriona, Milan 1983, 99.

All this shows that until human beings accept a different source of life free from nature, but which is manifested and realized in nature by transfiguring it – until then, we cannot overcome our tragic destiny.

8. *Living our humanity according to the life we have received*

At the Council of Ephesus, the Fathers declared that Mary gave birth to the Son of God according to human nature, and for this reason she is called *theotokos*, mother of God. The Council stressed that this child Mary generated is true man and true God. Now, if Jesus Christ is born of Mary as far as human nature is concerned, his self is the personal self of the Son of God. Christ has two natures, but as a person he is God, he is the Son of the Father. With this, the Council is affirming a very great truth about human beings themselves:[16] to be of 'true man', our human nature must be experienced by a self according to God, a filial self, an 'I' who has the life of God. To be 'true man', it is not so much about 'humanizing' us – this God has done in his Son. It is up to us to accept in our human nature the personal principle of existence, otherwise we risk remaining in a life according to 'our species', that is, according to our nature. And our nature groans and cries out, asking to be

---

16 The dogma, by giving us an understanding of humanity in its origins and its vocation, also has the task of protecting and expressing the divine life in humanity, if Christianity is "the imitation of the divine nature", according to the words of Gregory of Nyssa, *De professione christiana*, in Gregorii Nysseni Opera, VIII / 1, ed. Jaeger, Brill, Leiden 1952, 136, 2-8.

lived in a new way. It is precisely our nature that constantly acknowledges its inadequacy regarding life. It is precisely our nature that is stricken, slave to death, an easy prey for dark and malevolent forces. It is our nature to ask to be freed from the many tendencies towards evil that take possession of it in the darkness of the night, exposing it to bursts of false freedom, false power, false success, and then, tragically, cast it down to earth.

Through the covenant, God brought Abraham and Sarah to an *exodus* from this state of affairs in order for them to be disposed, through the art of welcome and acceptance, to receiving the life that God has prepared for them as a gift. And since the principle of life, hence of fatherhood, is our Father in heaven, Abraham will know, through his mysterious guest, that he is not to become a father by procuring his progeny, his descendants, through his own efforts, but to become a father through Sarah, who will give birth to a son. Until Abraham accepts Sarah as his 'other', he will insist on fatherhood according to his own view of things. Abraham must shift his attention to Sarah, as he learned to do earlier by slowly shifting his attention to God. And now, listening to God, he perceives that his fatherhood will not be his, but will be the work of God, through his relationship with Sarah which is no longer according to nature, but according to faith.

Following the example of Abraham and Sarah, we see the vision of humanity previously contemplated in the creation narrative, where the Lord presents Eve to Adam: human nature is created to be lived in a relational way. This is how the human being has been designed: the self is not an expression of nature, but is expressed through nature by living its relational truth, so that human nature lived in love with the other becomes the place of self-offering, of unity. Human realization, therefore, takes place in the world of the Spirit, because the way of existence of our nature according to relationship is possible only through participation in the divine life to which the Holy Spirit gives us access. And since human realization comes about by living human nature according to the filial self, the manner and fulfilment of this realization will consist in welcoming the gift of the Father, who is the Son. Whomsoever welcomes him will be given the power to become a child of God (cf. Jn 1:12).

Chapter 4
THE SPIRIT ENABLES US TO KNOW THE GIFT ACCORDING TO GOD

1. The individual takes possession of every gift and every grace

The problem of the individual self consists above all in using any gift that can be offered to it badly, because a self of this kind, while it might also have a certain notion of what relationship is, finds its epicentre in its own self, that is, a strong need that the self perceives as coming from its nature. And since this nature makes the self continually aware of its own shortcomings, it suffers from such shortcomings and consequently evaluates everything according to how useful it will be for itself. A dramatic example of this existential situation is described in Chapter 16 of the Book of the Prophet Ezekiel:

> On the day you were born your cord was not cut, nor were you washed with water to make you clean, nor were you rubbed with salt or wrapped in cloths. No one looked on you with pity or had compassion enough to do any of these things for you. Rather, you were thrown out into the open field, for on the day you were born you were despised.

"'Then I passed by and saw you kicking about in your blood, and as you lay there in your blood I said to you, "Live!" I made you grow like a plant of the field. You grew and developed and entered puberty. Your breasts had formed and your hair had grown, yet you were stark naked.

"'Later I passed by, and when I looked at you and saw that you were old enough for love, I spread the corner of my garment over you and covered your naked body. I gave you my solemn oath and entered into a covenant with you, declares the Sovereign Lord, and you became mine.

"'I bathed you with water and washed the blood from you and put ointments on you. I clothed you with an embroidered dress and put sandals of fine leather on you. I dressed you in fine linen and covered you with costly garments. I adorned you with jewellery: I put bracelets on your arms and a necklace around your neck, and I put a ring on your nose, earrings on your ears and a beautiful crown on your head. So you were adorned with gold and silver; your clothes were of fine linen and costly fabric and embroidered cloth. Your food was honey, olive oil and the finest flour. You became very beautiful and rose to be a queen. And your fame spread among the nations on account of your beauty, because the splendour I had given you made your beauty perfect, declares the Sovereign Lord.

"'But you trusted in your beauty and used your fame to become a prostitute. You lavished your favours on anyone who passed by and your beauty became his. You took some of your garments to make gaudy high places, where you carried on your prostitution. You went to him, and he possessed your beauty. You also took the fine jewellery I gave you, the jewellery made of my gold and silver, and you made for yourself male idols and engaged in prostitution with them. And you took your embroidered clothes to put on them, and you offered my oil and incense before them. Also the food I provided for you—the flour, olive oil and honey I gave you to eat—you offered as fragrant incense before them. That is what happened, declares the Sovereign Lord.

The prophet is talking about the people of the covenant, but this story could also be an anthropological photograph of the individual self, unable to grasp the real scope of relationship because it always reads everything in terms of itself. Its existential wound is a bottomless abyss, as Ezekiel attests, continuing with increasingly more serious episodes in this direction. The Prophet Hosea, also Psalm 78, depict a similar picture of the human situation, making us aware of the fact that Scripture notes the difficulty in helping human beings exit from such a situation. The texts quoted tell of the works that God has done for humankind and how human beings have misread them, have exploited them for themselves. As a result, these works did not help them grow in relationship, were not the opportunity for an *exodus* from slavery to a life of freedom. They did not transport humanity to a new level of existence, because even graces given were possessed as trophies by individuals, something to be used for their self-affirmation. The gift received does not become an opportunity to acquire wisdom, for new knowledge of the other as Giver and Saviour to mature, but remains closed within the individual's narrow horizons and, at the first trial we are again ready to cry for help. Someone like this never grows, never matures. For spiritual life, this is of extreme importance, because the culture in which we find ourselves has been based for centuries on the individual, always affirms individual values, and even believes that this is a cultural achievement.

But since the individual does not live spiritually, is not open to acknowledging human existence based on faith, it is very difficult to help him or her live at a new level of existence; they will be very adept at converting senses, meanings, words into their own perspective, and therefore it is always the individual in them who remains at the centre. The difference might be that instead of asserting themselves through a passionate and materialistic world, they do so through an idealistic, spiritualist, religious effort that offers salvation of itself without them needing to change. That is how the individual acts. Thus it may happen that individuals can understand even the most exquisitely spiritual and faith-based language, but interpret it in their terms, that is, interpret it as something that helps them to pass into eternity as individuals, just as they are. Yet there is one thing the individual fails to grasp existentially, and this is relationship as *ekstasis*, as a true exit from oneself. It is not grasped until it is acknowledged as one's own existence.

The most problematic point highlighted by these texts is that one cannot teach spiritual relationship to an individual, because what is learned will be reduced to a relationship according to nature. Ezekiel and Hosea are clear about this and, painfully, also Psalm 78.

All this speaks volumes about the difficulty of spirituality in our cultural and ecclesial context. For centuries our Christianity has been an individualist kind of Christianity, even when doing good, and asceticism has worked mainly on perfecting the individual. As a consequence, despite so much catechetical formation, so much spiritual and theological literature, we end up with a culture that is not only individualistic, but actually party to the decadence of individualism, i.e. subjectivism: the individual's view of things becomes an ideology whereby the individual subject demands a kind of attachment of the rest of the world to itself and its own views.

These results of our formation, quite the opposite to what we have been trying to achieve, pose radical questions about our approach to spirituality and our theological mentality. In fact, it is a mentality that does not contemplate a change, other than of ideas, whereas in Christian tradition theology has to do with divinization and this is not true if it does not adequately express the real *theōsis* of the theologian in the first instance. It comes down to thinking that by feeding human beings with good ideas, they will automatically become good; by teaching them about justice, they will act justly, until we realize that real life, which is unaltered by these ideas, does not begin even to change the ideas themselves. Not only do we not live as we think, but we start thinking about how we live.

This mentality of the individual so infiltrates our way of thinking about faith that we end up not even proposing a vision of communion anymore, but start out trying to adjust individuals so that they can experience the advantages of a social and community life. The individual needs others to live, but communion does not come to us spontaneously, and as individuals we build on the defences that protect us from the implicit danger that others represent for us. It is clear, in fact, that it is not according to human nature to live in communion, because communion is realized through self-sacrifice. But it does not belong to the nature of the individual to sacrifice himself or herself. If communion, which occurs only through self-sacrifice, belonged to the possibilities of human nature, the difficulties in living it would be moral, psychological or social. So, morals, psychology and sociology would be enough to resolve them. But this is not the case. For it to be possible, we would need to welcome that way of living – in a personal way – and that would no longer be an expression of our nature. So it has to be our mysterious identity generated through relationship which express itself in our nature. We receive this way of existing from God, because it is God's way of existing. Until individuals accept this way, they will make use of everything according to their individualistic, or even subjectivist perspective.

If individuals want to move to another level of existence which is no longer in the order of nature but in the order of the Spirit, that is, of love, of *agape*, then they must necessarily detach themselves from the way they currently live. It is about liberation from that state, saying goodbye to it. They are asked to sacrifice the state they are in. Without detachment from an individual consciousness totally conditioned by their nature, they cannot accept the new way of existing. The two ways of existing are actually incompatible with each other. Hence the need for the individual to die. The acceptance of life according to God means death to the individual and birth to a personal, communal existence. And when the individual begins to exist in a relational way which is no longer the expression of nature, but of relationship, a renewed human nature is the result, absorbed by and experienced in a relational self which finds its epicentre in the other.

2. *Faith and religion*

The great distinction between faith and religion comes into play here. Christian faith is not a religion, but a relational act, the recognition of the absolute value of the existence of the Other in whom we trust and on whom we recognize that we depend for our being, our existence.[1] Christianity is a way of existing in communion. Religion, on the other hand, is an expression of the individual, an individual's natural,

---

1 Cf. V. SOLOVIEV, *La critica dei principi astratti*, (or. Russian, Moscow 1877-1880) in ID., *Sulla Divinoumanità e altri scritti*, Jaca Book, Milan 1971, 203.

instinctive need just like the instinct to eat or cover oneself in order to protect oneself from the cold. The individual perceives that his life is endangered by so many elements and threatening forces that he cannot control. So he looks for a way to propitiate these forces and avail himself of some supernatural protection to preserve himself and survive. This gives rise to a set of very precise metaphysical certainties, a sort of creed, but as an ideology, identified with how it is formulated, so much so that fidelity to its literal truth guarantees the certainty of possessing the truth; it gives birth to a cult in which sacrifices are offered, inspired by a logic of exchange according to which the more valuable is the thing sacrificed or offered, the more God will be obliged to the one performing the sacrifice or offering; it generates an ethic that regulates daily behaviour, offering reassuring certainties to the self and guaranteeing the merit of individual virtue through its observance.[2] Religion is therefore a function of the individual. But Christ inaugurated a new life, not a new religion, and showed how all of life, in all its dimensions, is the place of communion with God, of thanksgiving, because life is given to human beings to make human life a life of communion with God. Here the individual is called to die in order to enjoy this life of communion which, as we have seen, is God's way of existing. And religion can be the last hiding place in which the individual self lurks so as not to have to give in and die.

---

2 On this, cf. CH YANNARAS *Against Religion*, Holy Cross Orthodox Press (September 15, 2013), though the text here is taken from the Italian translation, *Contro la religione*, cit.

3. *The person emerges from sacrifice according to faith*

In Chapter 22 of the book of Genesis, the Lord asks Abraham to offer his son Isaac as a holocaust. Abraham does not perform a religious act here. Formerly, the ancients offered their firstborn to God. Individuals at the time counted for little, and there would still be so many births in the family and the flock, to make up for the loss caused by sacrifice. Indeed, sacrifice was precisely a kind of tax paid to continue generating children by covering them with favours from the divinity. But Abraham had had Isaac by miraculous means. The sacrifice of Isaac, then, is the culmination of a life that is worthy of Abraham's title of 'father of us all' through faith (cf. Rom 4:16). The writer tells the story with particular attention to Abraham's promptness in leaving, and describes the journey to the mountain which, according to the word of the Lord, would be pointed out to him.

We are back in a situation we have already seen: God calling Abraham, asking something of him. The first time he asked him to leave his country, his homeland, his father's house and go toward a land that would be pointed out to him. Now we have practically the same scene put to us again.

> Some time later God tested Abraham. He said to him, "Abraham!"
>
> "Here I am," he replied.
>
> Then God said, "Take your son, your only son, whom you love—Isaac—and go to the region of Moriah. Sacrifice him there as a burnt offering on a mountain I will show you."

> Early the next morning Abraham got up and loaded his donkey. He took with him two of his servants and his son Isaac. When he had cut enough wood for the burnt offering, he set out for the place God had told him about.

The reader is assisted somewhat because the writer immediately explains that God is putting Abraham to the test, even if the meaning of the test will be visible only at the end. Now Abraham finally has his son. Sarah, his true wife, gave birth to him, and the two gained a son when both of them were no longer able to generate children, so that they would have the certainty that he was a gift from God. It was thanks to their acceptance of life as communion, thanks to welcoming the Lord who presented himself as a life of communion, and therefore a fruitful life, that they finally had a son. Certainly now Abraham feels fulfilled as a father; he can contemplate his progeny.

But the interpretation that Abraham puts on this gift is still according to an individual mentality, that is, he interprets the gift in terms of himself. Abraham looks at this child from a natural point of view and consequently is a father according to nature. But this is not the reality. Isaac is pure gift from God. However, since Abraham behaves towards this gift as a natural man, God makes himself felt once more. Abraham's *exodus* is to continue – from the individual to the person, from a state of life according to sin (which drives the human being back inside nature's needs) to arrive at a life according to the covenant, thus wholly dependent on the relationship whose epicentre is not Abraham's self but the other, that is, the Lord. Just as God has led him to consider Sarah from a perspective of true otherness, so now Abraham will have to rediscover his relationship with Isaac in terms of the covenant. Earlier, he had to achieve a real relationship with his wife, where the relationship was not a function of himself. Now he is called to do this with his son.

At first, Abraham could not have children because, out of fear for himself, he was ready to let Sarah pass as his sister. It was the consciousness of a self totally controlled by nature's vulnerability. Now the situation is new and, apparently, very different. The first time, Abraham was immediately ready to sacrifice Sarah to save himself. But now he is asked to sacrifice the son who had been promised him, for whom he had waited so long, and on whom he was so radically focused. At a first glance, it seems that Abraham's relationship to Isaac is a true relationship, because Isaac is the first in this relationship, and its epicentre. But evidently his individual self's consciousness is so pervasive that even his paternal relationship to his son is disguised. It might seem that Isaac was at the centre of everything, but in fact it is still a possessive relationship. The self can be self-affirming in order to free itself of the other, as Abraham had done with Sarah when they come to Egypt, or it can want to possess the other, experiencing the other as something it needs for itself. Isaac is someone Abraham needs for him to feel like a father. And if Isaac is a necessity for Abraham, then Abraham is a father according to nature and not according to the spirit, not according to faith. God is asking him to renounce this way of being a father according to nature. Just as God led

Abraham to discover a relationship with Sarah that was not according to nature – that is, one of kinship, being of the same flesh – but as true otherness, as a wife, so now he wants to lead him to see Isaac not according to nature, but as gift, that is, according to faith. In the sacrifice of Isaac, Abraham sacrifices his existence according to nature. We are approaching the completion of the covenant.

After a three day journey – the number three, a paschal number, the number of the triad, or surpassing the two – it is now that Abraham begins to enter the dimension of encounter:

> On the third day Abraham looked up and saw the place far away. Then Abraham said to his young men, "Stay here with the donkey; the boy and I will go over there; we will worship, and then we will come back to you." Abraham took the wood of the burnt offering and laid it on his son Isaac, and he himself carried the fire and the knife. So the two of them walked on together (vv. 4-6).

Abraham begins the ascent of the mountain with his son. The scene is eloquent. They are climbing the mountain of the holocaust. Abraham has loaded his son with the wood for the sacrifice but he has not told him that he is the one to be burned. Abraham is certainly going through a radical process of trusting the One who called him out of his father's house. In this ascent of the mountain, Abraham begins to abandon his habitual level of existence. He leaves the valley, is detached from the existence that everyone else has. His son follows him, because it is he who is the expression of this existence that Abraham must overcome and at the same time must rediscover. One kind of fatherhood according to nature must die and a fatherhood according to faith must appear. It is probable that they were climbing in daylight, but certainly Abraham would have recalled the stars he had counted one night, getting drunk on the incalculable numbers of the promise. Now his only son is carrying the wood on which he is to be set alight, and with him also the promise. For Abraham it is a question of existence. Finally, at the top of the mountain, the certainty emerges for Abraham that the truth is relationship, and that relationship is truth and that this truth concerns his fatherhood and his descendants, but that it is concealed in the other party to the relationship, the Lord, and therefore also in the other who is Isaac.

> Isaac said to his father Abraham, "Father!" And he said, "Here I am, my son." He said, "The fire and the wood are here, but where is the lamb for a burnt offering?" Abraham said, "God himself will provide the lamb for a burnt offering, my son." So the two of them walked on together.
>
> When they came to the place that God had shown him, Abraham built an altar there and laid the wood in order. He bound his son Isaac, and laid him on the altar, on top of the wood. (vv. 7-9).

The writer helps us to solve the drama of Abraham through his son. It is the son himself who is surprised that the sacrificial victim is missing, and he would certainly wonder why his father had not tried to find a lamb. Then he turns directly to his father, asking where the lamb is, since everything has been prepared for the sacrifice. But now Abraham has matured during his ascent. He is already responding according to the logic of the covenant, according to the relationship that is the truth of life. He tells himself that God himself will provide the lamb, and here lies Abraham's greatest prophecy. In fact, human beings will no longer offer sacrifice to God, but God the Father will sacrifice his own Son. A relational reality already begins to emerge from the text, which allows us to see one reality in another. Abraham will not sacrifice his son. Abraham will be the image of the Father who sacrifices his Son, the innocent Lamb who will enter into death so that humankind may live.

4. *In the sacrifice of his son, Abraham discovers fatherhood as love, the way God loves*

> Then Abraham reached out his hand and took the knife to kill his son. But the angel of the Lord called to him from heaven, and said, "Abraham, Abraham!" And he said, "Here I am." He said, "Do not lay your hand on the boy or do anything to him; for now I know that you fear God, since you have not withheld your son, your only son, from me." And Abraham looked up and saw a ram, caught in a thicket by its horns. Abraham went and took the ram and offered it up as a burnt offering instead of his son (vv. 10-13).

When Abraham raises the knife over his son, the vision of faith has matured in him. It is the knife raised over his son that has eliminated the old way of existence and made way for the new. On the altar a son was bound, one whom Abraham was master of according to nature, and now, after seeing the ram that the angel sends him to take the place of his son, he unties Isaac from the altar, receiving him as a son according to faith. God provides his own Son, who takes humanity's place so that human beings can live. In obedience to the One who had called him and brought him out of his land, from his father's house, Abraham died to his old life. In Isaac's sacrifice, Abraham's own sacrifice occurs, and therefore he discovers what God has called him to do. Only through sacrifice does he come to know the meaning of his vocation, his call, and discover fatherhood according to faith, according to the spirit. These are not two fatherhoods – one biological and the other spiritual. The greatness of the story of Abraham is revealed precisely in the overcoming of this dualism, because God leads him to understand that in biological fatherhood, in the fact that he really has a son Isaac, his fatherhood in faith is manifested, since it is precisely fatherhood according to faith that enabled him to generate Isaac according to the flesh. Fatherhood according to the Spirit is manifested in fatherhood according to nature, just as the person, being of the spiritual order, is expressed in nature because the Spirit integrates everything that exists. But Abraham now experiences and understands this unity of biological and spiritual fatherhood in obedience to the covenant, within an increasingly integral logic of relationship to which he abandons himself completely when climbing the mountain to sacrifice his son. It is there that he discovers self-sacrifice.

Abraham discovers this fatherhood when he gives precedence to the other, to the point of holding the knife over his son, which means holding the knife over himself. By killing his son, he would be killing himself as a father. But it is precisely within this sacrifice that Abraham contemplates the star-studded heavens. In fact, he understands that Isaac is not according to nature, but according to faith. And therefore, according to faith, the life of every new born is not a prolongation of humanity but a gift of the Father who is the source of all fatherhood. The human being born in faith lives life as a child. Abraham will be a father according to God's fatherhood. Therefore Abraham comes down from the mountain as the father of believers, as a father in faith. St Paul, citing Genesis 15:6, states that because he believed it was reckoned to him as righteousness (cf. Gal 3:6). Righteousness means that he has found a relationship according to truth, according to the harmony of the relationship with God through faith, because he has trusted, because he has shifted the epicentre of his life from self to the other. Thus he entered into a new mode of existence in the life of the Spirit.

Finally, we understand the meaning of the test that the narrator had announced to the reader in the first verse of Chapter 22. Why the test? The meaning of the test lies in understanding the gift. Abraham is put to the test so that he can discover the meaning of gift, which is the meaning of his vocation and the very meaning of his existence. Not according to the mentality of the individual self, according to the needs of nature, but according to the freedom of relationship. The meaning of the test is to let the human being see a life no longer lived according to the needs of nature, but according to freedom with the other. And since we know theologically that God's relationship is *agape*, gratuitous love, the test is to help the person understand gift as an experience of God's love. It is the experience of ourselves as testimony to God's love. The test is so that we can discover that we are the beloved of God, that God's love is expressed in us because God has called and chosen us as his 'you'. The meaning of the test is that self-consciousness becomes truly personal in every respect, according to God.

Once Abraham was so attached to himself that he was living as the centre of everything, so much so that he was ready to eliminate Sarah in order to save himself. Now he discovers that he is the centre of the other, because he is the centre of God, but in a totally new, free way. And he discovers that his son remains an epicentre, but also in a totally new way, because the same freedom that he experiences in his relationship with God he now experiences with his son.

This account of Abraham's story makes us understand that human beings are born into an existence that is not enough to make them live in such a way that they overcome the tragedy to which such existence is subjected. What has happened to human beings? Why do they handle this insufficiency more through injury, through what is missing, than what is there? What has happened that means human beings are controlled more by fear than by free creativity? Indeed, the strongest question that arises after Abraham is why we must go through sacrifice to begin living according to the God's way of existing, which is the only life worthy of us as human beings. In the accounts in Genesis 1-3, it is quite evident that the yearning for a life that corresponds to something other than what human beings find themselves living remains. It is understood that humanity's original vocation was very different from the existence we now lead. But it has taken the entire journey of Abraham's covenant to rediscover all its power and light.

5. *Unity is protected by love*

A possible difficulty is already hinted at in the description of the creation of humankind. Indeed, it is a potential drama that can end in real tragedy.

The anthropological vision that places the human being between earth and the sky, between creation and God, is widely known.[3] Now, this position, as we have seen, is exposed to the various 'isms' – from materialism to spiritualism – with which we try to explain the truth of humankind. But the very act of creation states that human beings belong to both worlds: God takes dust from the earth and then breathes on it. So the material from the first six days of creation is part of the human being, material that lives according to its reality, which Genesis describes with the expression 'according to its kind' (see Genesis 1:11,12,21,24,25, though the wording

---

3 Cf. IRENAEUS OF LYON, *Against Heresies*, III, 16,6; IV, 20,4; V.

varies, depending on which translation is being used), and that is beautiful. But there is also the breath of God in the human being, the breath which transmits the most intimate reality of God to this matter he has shaped. Humankind is this unity. Humankind is a being of unity *par excellence*, a reality that has its own nature, but which receives a new principle of life that wholly permeates the material of which it is made. So much so that the human body, animated by the breath of God, has practically nothing to do with the body of any other living being in creation. The human body is penetrated, vivified by an existence that is not typical of the material God took before he breathed on it. Once it has received this breath, this material is assumed into an existence in the image and likeness of God.[4]

What remains even after sin, and even if in a veiled manner, is the fact that the human being is a unity, a unified but composite organism. Now, it is important to understand this composition well, to know the reality of the human being more deeply. It is not a mixture of the material and immaterial or 'spiritual' world, as if the human being was made up simply of two realities, human nature and a kind of divine principle. The composition concerns the very manner of existence. The breath is life and at the same time the way in which the material that God had originally taken to shape the human being lives. The greatness of the human being lies not so much in the *what*, but in the *how* of existence. At this

---

4 "I, who am the creature of God, and bidden myself to be God": GREGORY OF NAZIANZEN, *Oration 43, funeral oration for Basil 48*.

point, St Irenaeus' vision of things helps us a lot, according to which God the Father shapes the human being with his two *hands – the Son and the Holy Spirit*,[5] which makes us understand even more that the creation of humankind will be definitively marked by God's way of existing. In fact the two hands represent the two personal existences through which the Father communicates himself. We can understand this breath that God has breathed into the human being against the background of this image of the two hands of the Father, as a sharing in God's relational existence through which the material that God has taken from creation is called to another destiny. It is as if, through humankind, the call to a life according to God's personal and communal existence was opened up for creation. Adam's vocation is to see that the cosmos is absorbed into the spiritual existence of God, which is his life. Thus, in the composition of the human being there is, on the one hand, a cosmic, palpable, corporeal reality. On the other there is only life itself, which expresses itself through its way of living and experiencing cosmic reality according to the way of existing of the two hands – the Son and the Spirit – that is, a relationship oriented to the Father. The hand of the Son will be the filial imprint which guarantees that the human being can live in the manner of the Son, in the manner of divine humanity, receiving life in a manner according to God. The hand of the

---

5 "… as if He did not possess His own hands. For with Him were always present the Word and Wisdom, the Son and the Spirit, by whom and in whom, freely and spontaneously, He made all things" IRENAEUS OF LYON, *Against Heresies*, Book 4, Chap. 20, 1.

Holy Spirit, who is the Lord of *koinōnia*, communicates this life of God as a foundational relationship for humankind, that is, the relationship between the Son and the Father. The Holy Spirit is the breath of the Father and of the Son, he is the life between them, the Love of love. Therefore he guarantees that humankind will have an existence of filial love toward the Father.

As we have seen, immediately after the creation of Adam, God sees the man's being alone as something 'not good' for him. He then draws the other from Adam, causing a sort of split in human nature between masculine and feminine as a way of assisting it to live according to this existence received from the breath and the two hands with which it had been shaped. God creates them as two and, in the search for each other – Eve looking for the place from which she had been taken, Adam looking for his missing rib[6] – God hides the breath with which he shaped Adam. Placed before each other, they discover the help they need to live the life that John would call *zoē*, which is typical only for God. Eve is taken from Adam as a 'helper' (cf. Gen 2:20), that is, a helper in existing according to God, according to relationship, according to the search for the other. The life that is expressed in this masculine and feminine division of nature is a continuous call to the divine life destined to be realized in them. Eve, taken from Adam, can only consider her relationship with Adam to be primary, and Adam can only find the epicentre of his relationship in Eve, because

---

6 Cf. S Bulgakov, *Unfading Light*, though taken here from the Italian translation, *La luce senza tramonto*, cit., 329.

otherwise he is not whole. Adam can no longer exist without union with Eve, without striving for unity with her. Human beings will no longer be fulfilled alone, because the life they have received makes them essentially relational.

Now, it is precisely this human makeup – as a reality of nature and this nature's mode of existence – that is vulnerable. The temptation described in Chapter 3 of Genesis is one which strikes at the unity between nature and this nature's way of being.

Eve is created as a helper for a relational existence, so that the man does not live as an individual, but as a person. And the temptation strikes precisely at this relationship. It directly affects the foundational relationship, the one with God, which it redirects toward creation, that is, to the material God used to shape Adam, the man. The temptation acts on the way in which this nature is lived: it cleverly urges them to become the epicentre of the relationship. He who communicated his breath, that is, the Father of the two hands, no longer holds first place in the relationship. It is communion that is being attacked as a mode of existence, and the result is a relationship no longer according to God but according to nature, that is, where one tries to take possession of things and people. From now on the world must belong to the two of them, so that they may feel like God. At first they had received existence from God, together with a way of existing according to God. Now they project onto the tree [of knowledge of good and evil] characteristics that in themselves belong only to God (see Gen 3:6). Thus an idolatrous relationship is born, which in reality is no longer a relationship as such but an illusion that they are relating. So much so that immediately the relationship between the man and the woman is also broken. A kind of war between the sexes begins: the woman will try to seduce the man and the man will try to dominate the woman. And life will no longer be according to God, but already according to passion, therefore according to nature.

By yielding to this temptation, which is a direct attack on life lived as a relationship, tragedy takes place. What was first perceived as a veiled possibility now ruptures human identity, which begins to divide between the material and the spiritual, between the corporal and the spiritual. Once the way of existing according to the Spirit has been extinguished, what remains is an existence according to nature but with ongoing anguish, because it changes the perception that the self has of itself: from an absolutely personal reality, based on the consciousness of self in the Spirit, it becomes an experience of insufficiency, shortcoming. Therefore it is a consciousness marked by pain, by the fear of failure.

The human being cannot accept this and tries every way possible to rekindle what has been extinguished, meaning the way of relational existence according to the Spirit. But the human being can no longer grasp the true meaning of relationship. Unconsciously we think of relationships as a promise of life, but at the same time they are a painful thing, precisely because a sort of perversion of relationship has taken place which causes the epicentre to always shift in favour of the self.

6. *From the personal to the individual self*

Yet the true self remains. Human beings cannot completely return to a life only according to nature. And this is what hell is for the human being – not accepting a life lived only according to nature and its demands, yet without the possibility of rising to a life which is superior to nature, one which enables the human being to appropriate human nature freely. The hell of this self is therefore the lack of freedom. The self will never be free of itself, because its consciousness is nailed to the needs of nature. At the same time, however, human beings are still able to grasp that this manner of existence could be altered if relationship were to be recovered, or in other words, if love enters the scene, enabling them to overcome their isolated individuality and join with with others. Here there is huge room for possibilities in which the Spirit blows and only the Father knows how and in what ways people can find themselves living what is God's way of existing. It is such a personal space of the Father that it is beyond us and remains impenetrable to our understanding. We are dealing with a mystery that the Son himself has given to us, emphasizing that certain things were not even entrusted to him, but only belong to the Father (cf. Mk 13:32, Mt 24:36). This is especially beautiful because we begin to grasp that there is a personal existence, not of necessity, but of freedom, because where there is love, things shift in favour of free relationship.

What characterizes the work of the Spirit in this humanity that has lost its true way of existing is charity, because where the Spirit breathes, humanity perceives this as charity. Wherever the wind of the Holy Spirit blows there is a flourishing, an opening to life, because the first sign of life according to the Spirit is openness. Openness, welcome, acceptance – here lies charity's first step.

This reminiscence of a manner of relational existence in the human being is attested to in Chapter 25 of the Gospel of Matthew where three parables are narrated that somehow open up a vision of the end of history. First of all there is the parable of the ten virgins awaiting the bridegroom – evidently addressed to the people of the covenant who are the only ones waiting in expectation of the Bridegroom of humanity, the Messiah. Then there is the parable of the talents, addressed to the people of the Son, to whom He has delivered the benefits of the kingdom, and who will be judged on the basis of what they have done with such benefits – the benefits of the life he has given. And finally there is a kind of parable, the story of the Last Judgement, where the king will call those who sit on his right hand 'blessed by my Father' (Mt 25:34). They can enjoy the kingdom prepared for them because they have given food, drink, clothing to the Lord. Clearly this story is addressed to those who have not known the Lord, so much so that they tell him: *'Then the righteous will answer him, "Lord, when was it that we saw you hungry and gave you food, or thirsty and gave you something to drink? And when was it that we saw you a stranger and welcomed you, or naked and gave you clothing? And when was it that we saw you sick or in prison and visited you?" And the king will answer them, "Truly I tell you, just as you did it to one of the least of these who are members of my family, you did it to me"* (vv. 37-40).

What remains in the human being, in the perception of the self, even if it is an individual perception linked to biological existence is, at any rate, a relational consciousness in which the Spirit can blow and germinate charity, so that human beings can do good to others as they would like it to be done to themselves. These will be recognized by the Father. The way in which this happens is reserved to the Father. Whether a person has been doing this for years or makes a single gesture, it is reserved to the Father. But it is said that the Lord does not recognize those who do not understand this spirit that leads to charity, openness, acceptance, because they have not recognized the needy. These scenes are repeated throughout the Gospels, where we find tight-fisted characters who will be buried along with their possessions, like the rich man who does not see Lazarus (see Lk 16:19-31). In fact, thanks to the existence of of the communion that God extends to human beings, we cannot relate to God if we do not relate to others. But the reverse also applies: those who are moved by a Spirit they do not know, but who warm hearts and make charity germinate, those who make gestures of love toward their fellow human beings have done these things to God.

But the most tragic aspect underlined by the Gospels regarding humanity which has fallen to the level of the individual, and is thereby deprived of personal awareness, is when human beings seek to recover the relational world through religion. As we have seen, religion is a natural function that belongs to the instinct of preservation. Just as other needs are innate, so too is the religious path individuals set out on to save themselves. It is clearly an illusion because individuals will try to live their religion worthily, deploying all their efforts to accomplish what is prescribed, consider how it was established, and save themselves through their own virtuous efforts. Salvation here is conceived of as resulting from the individual. But since it is really about discovering a personal, relational, communal way of living founded on the Spirit, individuals cannot do it alone. It is not a question of adding something to ourselves, but of changing the way we exist. And this change does not happen by commanding our will to realize communion, committing ourselves to communion. Instead, communion is the very way we live. It is not an addition to individual life, a conquest of one's commitment. It is precisely the very life of the self lived in such a way as to lived communally. So it makes no sense to strive for relationships, because, as we have seen in the story of Abraham, the epicentre of the self cannot shift without God's intervention. Therefore one of the most dramatic images is the rich young man who asks Jesus what he must do to achieve eternal life (see Mt 19:16-22). When Christ quotes the commandments concerning relationship to others, the young man says that he has already accomplished all this since childhood. Yet he still lacks life, and in the end he leaves sad, because he trusts more in what he has and what he can do rather than in what Christ can give him.

We also have the opposite example. It is surprising that, precisely in the Gospel of Matthew, which most respects the tradition of the covenant people, the Messiah was first found by foreigners, because they were obedient and docile seekers (see Mt 2:1-12). They did not seek confirmation for themselves, and their search is a typical example of the openness that can only be aroused by the breath they received, then setting out on a long journey, a long exodus. And when they arrived at the encounter, they went back by another road, because their life had changed.

Chapter 5
THE BEGINNING OF THE SPIRITUAL LIFE

1. Christ's sacrifice

So that the human being can recover a way of being worthy of the creature made in the image and likeness of God, the Father sends his Son who became man through the Holy Spirit and the involvement of the Virgin of Nazareth. God does not work salvation from the outside. Abraham's covenant journey is a long preparation of waiting, trials, ascents and falls for the favourable time to mature for the entrance of the Messiah.

Abraham's point of arrival – that is, a life according to the covenant, hence a relational existence – is the image of what God the Father will accomplish in his Son as a true and real change in human existence. In the Son, the Father will elevate humanity to a filial existence, not as an external intervention but by assuming human nature in the person of the Son. In the Son, humanity is lived in a communal, filial way, as a gift of self. Through the Incarnation, the Son of God lives as a man, and therefore can see death which lies ahead as the insurmountable limit of human nature. And it is precisely the acceptance of death that amounts to the fulfilment of humanity's redemption, because the Son will make death – the result of mortality present throughout the course of a life of isolation and separation – an event of communion with the Father and with human beings. Precisely because of his communion with the human race, the consequences of the assumption of humanity's sinfulness by Christ also had to extend to his physical existence. But since he was sinless, death was not a necessity for him: he took it on voluntarily, offering his life as a supreme and final sacrifice to God: 'No one takes it [life] from me, but I lay it down of my own accord' (Jn 10:18). The Son of God, through his sacrifice of love, the gift of life, gives an unprecedented meaning to death. What, up to that point was separation between humanity and God, and dominated all human beings so that, fearful for themselves, they were hostile to and in conflict with others (see Heb 2:14-15), Christ will convert into the supreme manifestation of God as the one who gives himself, thus removing the poison out of death so that it is no longer the principle of hatred and separation among people but, through Christ's sacrifice, acquires the meaning of a passing into something, and unity. So, in Christ, death too is experienced according to God's way of existing, in relational terms.[1]

---

1 Nicolas Cabasilas states that there are three obstacles separating humanity from God: nature, sin or will corrupted by evil, and death: "The first was taken away by the Saviour through his incarnation, the second through his crucifixion, since the cross destroys sin ... and finally, he breaks down the last wall through his resurrection, completely banishing the tyranny of death from human nature": NICOLAS CABASILAS, *La vita in Cristo*, III, i (*PG* 150, 572CD). In English as *The Life in Christ*, St Vladimir's Seminary Press; Ex-Monastery Library edition (March 1, 1997).

But why was sacrifice necessary?

It takes sacrifice because the death of a human being has taken place, and death has remained the unbridgeable abyss between human beings and God. As we have already seen, there is no way human beings can overcome this abyss alone. There is no escape in the face of death that can save us. There is a need for someone to come and rescue us. This is the grand vision of the Father, who sends his Son from his eternal home to become one of us. Then from within the human perspective, he experiences death in relationship, in obedience of love for the Father (cf. Jn 14: 31). There can be no bridge to bypass death in order to overcome it. We have to go through it. And the only one who can do this is someone who knows that behind death there is nothing but the Father. But since death created division between human beings, conflict, killing each other to save themselves, the Son of God enters into death, going through it in relation to the Father who offers him into the hands of human beings. He finds these hands that kill his Son. While we were still sinners, he delivered himself into our hands (cf. Rom 5:8,10). It is clear then that his handing over of himself is accomplished through his being killed, and in our discovery of God as the love that is given in this way.

Sacrifice was therefore necessary because it took someone to give meaning to death, overcoming it through the relationship which allows humanity to pass through death to the Father. We needed sacrifice because we had to

"Therefore, from then on there was no further impediment for us to share in his graces, except sin" (*Ibidem* 572C).

enter into the death of humanity, take it on from within in a relationship of filial love, for it to lead to the Father.

The Father's plan is to give us his Son as a gift. This Son who takes upon himself the tragic destiny of Adam. But it is precisely because he lives his humanity according to the divine manner of existence – that is, he lives his human nature as a person, not as an individual – he assumes all of human nature in its entirety into his relationship with the Father. This means that he surrenders to the Father and surrenders to the evil of the world, to the rapacious hands of fallen humanity, all in the same action. Fallen humanity needs revenge, needs to vent its anger, which does not admit its sin but identifies a culprit on whom to load it all. The Son takes all this. And in this sacrifice the whole of humanity passes to the Father who forgives us on the cross and also cleanses the killers, so that all may be treated in a personal way, with mercy, love, benevolence. In this priestly sacrifice which unites humanity to the Father in the manner of the Son, in an obedience of love, redemption and the rebirth of humanity takes place. When Christ breathes his last on the cross, when all humankind has become gift in him, this humanity receives his breath and begins to live in a filial way. In the death of Christ, sinful humanity separated from God also dies. In reality, it was a humanity that had already died because human existence was not life, but was simply waiting for death, manifested itself as death and produced death. It brought about the death of the Son of God. It was a life that was quite incapable of accepting the Gift. Only in the sacrifice of the Gift, that is of the Son, is humanity regenerated. While humanity is rejecting the Gift, the Gift is regenerating humanity and making it into gift. The life of human beings regenerated in Christ is a life constituted by the same Spirit who enables the Son to live in communion with the Father. Therefore in human beings too, he lives as communion between the Son and the Father (cf. 1 Cor 1:9).

A regenerated humanity is baptized by the washing of water and the Spirit from the pierced side. It is the Father who gathers up the Son in the sacrifice offered in the Spirit (cf. Heb 9:14) and raises him up. His body, his human nature are no longer opaque because they no longer carry death within themselves. They can no longer be subject to the sin of the world. The resurrection of the Lord's flesh, in which new divine-human spiritual sensations are at work, is the recasting of human nature, the realization and revelation of the perfect humanity.[2] Humanity alone cannot be considered perfect, complete and true, because humanity's union with God is not something complementary, accessory, but a constituent element of it, since humanity was created in the image of God, that is, to share in divine life. Christ, who died once and for all, made perfect those he sanctified through his sacrifice (cf. Heb 10:14). Then, as the Gospel of John says in Jesus' farewell discourse, it is to our advantage that he goes to the Father (cf. John 16:7), that he drinks the Paschal cup and eats the Passover meal, because this way his

---

2 " ... the Saviour alone was the first and only one to reveal the true and perfect man": NICOLAS CABASILAS: *The Life in Christ*. St Vladimir's Seminary Press; Ex-Monastery Library edition (March 1, 1997), though taken here from the Italian translation, *La vita in Cristo*, IV, X (*PG* 150, 680C).

body will no longer be his alone; it will become the dwelling with many places (cf. Jn 14:2) .³

2. Born into Easter

In baptism we are grafted into this resurrected body in order to live no longer subject to sin and death, but free as children. If before, self-consciousness felt the evil within, the emptiness and the threat that came from sin and death (cf. Rom 7:17), now the human being is inhabited by the Spirit (cf. Rom 8:9). Through the body of Christ we are put to death (cf. Rom 7:4) to everything that was the culture and the way of being of the individual, including the law of religion with which human beings sought to save themselves, and we are resurrected with him (cf. Rom 6:5-6), have passed into his resurrected body. In this way we can interpret the sacrament of baptism as humanity's true participation in Christ's Pasch from within the person of the Son. By truly experiencing

---

3   "... the blessed flesh of the Lord is precisely *the Church*. In fact with the coming of the Spirit, the 'Lord's Body' was revealed as Church and, from then on, is the space where the faithful experience the new spiritual life and where salvation becomes real. In this body which is the Lord's Body, the spiritual life of the Head reaches all its members and enlivens them ... Christ is not simply a redeemer who, after having redeemed people then abandons them to themselves and entrust his wise teaching to them: much more radically, he creates a space for new action by people. And this space is his body": P NELLAS *Deification in Christ: the Nature of the Human Person*, Contemporary Greek Theologians (Book 5) series, St Vladimirs Seminary Press; First Edition edition (June 17, 1987), though taken here from the Italian translation, *Voi siete dei. Antropologia dei Padri della Chiesa*, (or. Greek, Athens 1981), Città Nuova, Rome, 136.

death to a way of existing, we awaken in the risen body of the Lord to a new life, enabled to exist according to the Son. In other words we have to encounter God the Father as dead people, and in this encounter, our resurrection takes place.

The place of this encounter is the body of the risen Christ. This is why the Lord says, '*It is to your advantage that I go away*' (Jn 16:7). For it is to our great advantage not to walk beside or behind Christ, as the apostles did in Palestine, but within him as the one who died and is risen. Furthermore, with this, even the Holy Spirit who was 'near us' has now come 'into us' (cf. John 14:17). Now we have the Spirit who enables us to recognize that we are children, because he enables us to relate to God as Father. It is then that the shift has been truly accomplished. We died as individuals and we rose again as people according to the existence of God. And we begin to live in Christ, where we learn to live in one another, just as the Lord says: '*On that day you will know that I am in my Father, and you in me, and I in you*' (Jn 14:20); "*As you, Father, are in me and I am in you, may they also be in us*' (cf. Jn 17:21). By being grafted onto Christ, we begin to learn to live in the other.[4]

---

4 "After Jesus' return to the Father, the Holy Spirit made room in men's hearts for the transfigured Lord. Now he is in us and we in him – again in the Holy Spirit ... To be a "neighbour" in the Christian sense means to suspend the I-not-you, mine-not-thine evil consequences of blurred or lost individuality and dignity. Genuine love of neighbour is impossible through human strength alone: it necessitates something new which comes from God and which surpasses the logic of mere human differentiation or unification: the love of the Holy Spirit among men. Christian love does not attempt to fuse the I and the you or to impose on them

Being baptized in Christ means being immersed in him and remaining in him. In John 15, when Christ says that he is the true vine and we the branches, in practice he is describing the pattern of the new human being totally united to Christ, living Christ's life because he remains in his love. As Ezekiel states (cf. 15:1-6), the wood of the vine, when it does not bear fruit, serves no purpose except to be burned. You cannot make things with it as you can with the wood of other plants. But its true fruit is not the cluster of grapes nor the single grape – it is the wine. This wood has something that generates a juice when the water passing through it gives it life, and this juice is expressed as fruit – the grapes – that have all they need in them to become wine. But, in order for the grapes to become wine, they have to pass through the wine-press, that is to say Easter, death, the gift of self. Only in this way does it become sweet must, which with patience, time, matures as wine. Christ is practically saying that the meaning of the vine is wine, which in the Wisdom texts is love, the true taste of life (cf. Sir 31:27). Thus human nature finds its unique meaning exclusively if it is lived in a personal, that is, a filial, relational way. Only then does it bear fruit, which is love. But, to bear fruit, this humanity must live in a communal way, so it must pass through the Easter triduum to die to an individual way of living and rise again to a relational life.

an attitude of selflessness that would annihilate the individual. It is the disposition of reciprocal openness and autonomy together, that simultaneous intimacy and dignity which comes from the Holy Ghost." R GUARDINI *The Lord*, Gateway editions (from original 1954 Regnery Publishing), 2016 Impression, 508-509.

But we cannot pass through the Easter triduum except with the Son. It is not possible to experience the meaning of death, sacrifice, as individuals. The hero's sacrifice leads nowhere, does not remove anything of humanity in life. Instead, it is necessary to truly enter into full participation in the life of the Son to have the Holy Spirit within. Then humanity is able to produce grapes and sustain sacrifice in Christ, the gift of self, and move on to the Father as risen beings.

In baptism, life as an expression of our nature dies. This life is like the wood of the vine, and serves only to let the Holy Spirit pass through it, making humanity live by producing the fruit that is love. We are grafted into Christ and his life – that is, the Holy Spirit, communion with the Father – passes through us, flows within us, penetrates all of our humanity and makes it live in such a way as to bear fruit. And here we must be careful not to identify the fruit simply with the works that human beings can do. The fruit is our living and acting in a loving way, according to the gift of self, that is, it includes the paschal mystery. Just as the true fruit of the vine is not the grape but the wine, so the Holy Spirit who makes us live in the Son as children makes us continually follow the whole of the Son's journey to its completion. So the Easter Triduum is included as part of the journey of every human being who experiences this sinful history as a child of God. Life in the Holy Spirit is the path humanity follows when lived this way. From now on, human life will be in the footsteps of the Christ of the Gospels: from the cave in Bethlehem, in which we recognize ourselves as neophytes, until leaving the empty tomb, because everything that is lived in love is snatched away from corruption and death and enveloped in the eternal love of the Father who does not let anything slip into the grave.

3. *From the individual self to the self lived as communion*

Spiritual life begins in the true sense of the term when communion appears in human existence, when we receive as a gift the life that is constituted as communion, as a relationship according to God. Spiritual life really begins only when all that is typically human begins to be freed from the grip of the self-affirming rapacious self, to be lived as a free relationship. Spiritual life begins when all human nature is delivered to self in communion. If 'person' means the unity of a loving, relational principle, a relational self-consciousness that expresses life in its human nature as communion, then spiritual life is only possible for persons.

It is clear that this is a journey that will end in the kingdom of God, because if the person emerges from communion, in a certain sense it is an eschatological reality belonging to the kingdom of heaven, where we will fully experience communion because all the barriers that divide us from others will fall. Then God will give us that 'white stone' on which our name is written (cf. Rev 2:17). Then we will experience being a person of and toward the future, which does not mean that we cannot experience it in some way right from now. Only that life now is the gestation of the new human being created according to God, similar to that which leads the embryo through the darkness of the womb.[5]

This preparation is brought about through our amalgamation with the body of Christ.[6]

We can thus conclude that spiritual life is the ecclesial existence of man. It therefore does not articulate or establish itself as a path typically marked out by religion, but as the manifestation of a new existence of humanity which, in history, is realized as ecclesial life – the Church as communion.[7]

The meaning of the spiritual life is to live our humanity as a theophany, as a manifestation of God's love. How then

---

5 "This world leads the new, inner man created according to God, through gestation to the point where he is moulded, shaped and become perfect and generated to the perfect world, where he never grows old. It is like the embryo which, while in a dark and fluid existence, is being prepared by nature for life in light and plasma, almost taking its future existence as the norm, just like the saints; this is the meaning of the Apostle's words to the Galatians: "My little children, for whom I am again in the pain of childbirth until Christ is formed in you" NICOLAS CABASILAS, *The Life in Christ*. St Vladimir's Seminary Press; Ex-Monastery Library edition (March 1, 1997), though taken here from the Italian translation, *La vita in Cristo*, I, i (*PG* 150, 496BC). Cf. also DIADOCO DI FOTICA, *Definizioni. Discorso ascetico diviso in cento capitoli pratici di scienza e discernimento spirituale*, 88, in *La Filocalia*, I, Gribaudi, Turin 1983, 386-387.

6 "The birth which is baptism is the beginning of the future life, the acquiring of new limbs and new senses and preparation for existence beyond; but it is not possible to prepare ourselves for the future age in any other way than by accepting the life of Christ here and now, Christ who *is the father of the future age* just as Adam is of the present": NICOLAS CABASILAS, *La vita in Cristo*, II, v (*PG* 150, 541A).

7 Cf. CH YANNARAS *Contro la religione*, cit.

is spiritual life to be found in a human being? The infallible verification of authentic spiritual life is its manifestation of God's love for humankind in our way of thinking, feeling, in our will and our concrete bodily gestures. Just as Christ showed God's love for a humanity that lived an existence marked by death, so in every Christian the life of Christ that accepted in baptism and that Christ extends over him – that is, the Holy Spirit – moves him to perform the same constitutive act of his redemption, that is, Easter. The Christian has been constituted in the Easter of Christ, and fulfils his or her life in the same paschal mystery. The measure of the authenticity of spiritual life is life lived as a gift. In other words, 'be merciful just as your Father is merciful' (Lk 6:36). If mercy is the gesture by which God covers the distance between himself and dead humanity, spiritual life allows Christians to continue to cover the space that divides the suffering human being, the sinner, suffocated in the individual, from the existence of communion which is the Church. The Church is not primarily an institution, but the epiphany of the new creation, of this new way of existence brought back and offered to the love of God and to communion with him.

After centuries in which the Church has been structured according to a para-imperial and para-state form, there is also a great commitment of the spiritual life today in freeing Christians from a sterile scaffolding, to make the Church emerge as existence in the communion of a humanity which aims to cover the distances of the loneliness and suffering of isolated human beings.

Clear signs of spiritual life are charity, mercy, acceptance of the other, life free from selfishness, ethnocentrism and idolizing a particular culture or history; it is also showing that we belong to a community where life is expressed as communion. Other essential signs of the spiritual health of Christians are when, through baptism, they overcome relationships linked only to nature, such as blood and family relationships, and show that they belong to communion adopted in freedom.

Yet the ability of Christians to manifest and reveal life as communion has become blurred since, in the course of history, many of the things which baptism should have changed for people have re-entered the Church's communion. The more we are able to truly manifest spiritual life, therefore to overcome this mentality of the natural order, the more our life will become a continuous revelation of the other. The more deeply we are aware that our lives are founded on Christ, the more our action and our way of being will manifest it.

Chapter 6
LIFE IN CHRIST

1. To the Father, through Christ, in the Holy Spirit

To perceive oneself as united to Christ, indeed, as a part of him, is prayer, certainly one of the fundamental spiritual dimensions which follows on from baptism. To pray means to live one's life in relation to the Father, through Christ, in the Holy Spirit who continually shapes our filial mentality. It is a state of dialogue, an overcoming of loneliness and isolation. Prayer is the expression of the new life we have received, a life that is affirmed in Christ and lived with Christ and in him. Prayer cannot be treated, just like spiritual life itself, as starting from our humanness as such, but only from the gift received.

The life received is life which, in the Holy Spirit, moves and is realized in relationship with the Father. Since the only humanity that can live in relationship with the Father is that of the Son, the spiritual life is accomplished in the Son and prayer can be none other than the inner articulation of this relationship. And since we become children through baptism, prayer is the expression of baptismal filial life and is the fundamental characteristic of this new existence that we receive in the baptismal washing.[1] After baptism, human

1 Prayer, says Gregory of Sinai, is "the revelation of baptism"

beings no longer perceive themselves as individuals and therefore no longer consider prayer as the effort to get in touch with God, to reach up to his level. Prayer by now is the fundamental dimension of this new human situation. It is like the breath of life. In life according to nature we say someone is dead when they cease breathing. The same is true for life according to the Spirit. If this state of dialogue is interrupted, this filial consciousness, this perception of the communal self, this essential need to communicate, talk to one another, meet each other, disclose oneself to the other, be shaped by the Other who is the Father, it is already death. Therefore, spiritual death is verified when prayer ceases, just as it also is when charity and acceptance cease.

Spiritual life holds together with everything else. It is not possible to note intense prayer and at the same time the absence of mercy and charity that inspire a person to be closer to those who suffer from any evil. The coexistence of frequent and prolonged prayer is not possible if we are locked into a mentality according to nature, locked into ethnocentrism, our social, economic circumstances, etc. These discrepancies are possible in the devotional practices of a religious mentality, where human beings decide to perform the exercises prescribed by religious ascetic practice, but they cannot exist within an ecclesial path of

---

(*Capita de ascesi per acrostichidem*, 113: PG 150, 1277D). It is not an alternative to the normal sacramental life of the Church, but precisely the means by which sacramental grace awakens within us. Cf. also DIADOCO DI FOTICA, *Definizioni. Discorso ascetico diviso in cento capitoli pratici di scienza e discernimento spirituale*, 77, cit., 378-379.

faith characterized by the acceptance of life, and therefore by letting this life flow through one in order to to live one's nature in a relational, communal way. Thus in ancient times it was strongly emphasized that it all begins with the gift received, the objectivity of the gift which constitutes a new existence. We could not pray the Our Father if we did not come out of the baptismal waters, because before, lacking the life of the Son, not having the Holy Spirit who is communion with the Father, praying the Our Father was a nominalistic exercise.[2] I cannot say 'Father' if I am not a son and I cannot say 'our' if I do not experience any relationship with my brothers and sisters, except those related by blood or my ethnic group. When commenting on the rites of Christian initiation, St Augustine, like many other Fathers of the Fourth Century, underlines how the Creed is given those preparing for baptism as a sign of recognition by Christians who are expressing their own life.[3] The others who are not living what is expressed in the Creed

---

2 "Baptism has become a new mother for us, and through her we have become children of the Father, and we can call him 'Our Father' with love ... From Eve we were dust and children of death, from this new mother we are children of God. From now on we have a Father in heaven to whom we can confidently address ourselves as 'our Father' ... If the procreation of Eve still had value, our 'father' would be in Sheol, and not in heaven": GIACOMO DI SARUG, ed. Bedjan, *Homiliae selectae Mar-Jacobi Sarugensis*, I, Paris-Leipzig 1905, 198. Cit. in S. BROCK, *The Holy Spirit in the Syrian Baptismal Tradition*, The Syrian Churches Series 9, Jacob Vellian Ed., Kottayam 1998, 88-89.

3 AUGUSTINE, *Serm.* 212, 2; 213, 2; 214, 1-2, in *Opere di sant'Agostino* 32/1, Città Nuova, Roma 1984, 199-201, 205, 219-221.

will consider it only on a notional level, therefore with the danger of making it the object of rational discussion, but not as the expression of spiritual truths. In ancient times the objective, ontological aspect of the newness of baptismal life was stressed so much that St Ambrose also points out to the neophytes that until they have the life of the Son, he could not explain the sacraments and the great contents of faith to them, but could only speak of the great figures of the Old Testament to get them used to entering the life of their ancestors and arouse in their hearts a kind of desire for a new way of existing.[4]

It follows from this that every exercise of the spiritual life is the expression of our being rooted in Christ, of our familiarity with the Holy Spirit. There is a close correspondence between the sacramental journey and the path of spiritual life, so much so that one could say that spiritual life is the increasingly fuller awareness of sacramental life.[5] Christian life is the journey from baptismal grace secretly present in the heart to baptismal grace experienced with full awareness. Living in Christ means accessing the fullness of his grace that inaugurated a new state of creatureliness. Since we are generated by the Church in baptism, it is there that the source of life that is the foundation of all human existence in Christ is found. Cyril of Jerusalem, citing Thales, says that 'The water was the beginning of the world,' and then

---

4 AMBROSE, *De mysteriis*, 1 (*PL* 16, 389; SC 25bis, 156).
5 Cf. P EVDOKIMOV, *La conoscenza di Dio secondo la tradizione orientale*, Italian tr. (or. Fr., Lyon 1967) Paoline, Rome 1983, 104-105.

adds 'and Jordan the beginning of the Gospel tidings.'[6] By immersion in the baptismal font, the neophyte receives the principle of being[7] which determines the spiritualization of all sensible reality, allowing us to directly know the things of God which have become immanent to the spirit.

This also leads to an understanding from which every simply conceptual manner is excluded, but it is an organic, all-encompassing experience where everything becomes the mediation of a unique, integral life.

All the sacraments the Church celebrates express and realize the unity of our human reality with the life of the Son in an ontological way, and are therefore 'instruments of unity.'[8] Therefore also a personal act of charity done by

---

6 *Catechesi*, III, 5, in Cyril and John of Jerusalem, *Catechesi prebattesimali e mistagogiche*, Paoline, Milan, 1994, 192. The text can be found online in English, e.g. at http://classicalchristianity.com/2011/11/16/st-cyril-on-water/.

7 "[In baptism] we exchange life with Life: we give one and, in its place, we receive another. But while the gift of our life is but a figurative and symbolic death, our regeneration is indeed Life": NICOLA CABASILAS, *Commento della divina liturgia*, 4, Italian tr. by AG NOCILI, *Messaggero*, Padua 1984, 71-72.

8 "The sacraments, being the means of salvation, must be understood as instruments of unity. By realizing, restoring or reinforcing the union of man with Christ, they realize, re-establish or reinforce, by this very fact, his union with the Christian community. And this second aspect of the sacrament, the social aspect, is so intimately united with the first, which can sometimes be said to be equally good, or even in certain cases it must rather be said that the Christian unites himself with Christ through his union with the community": H DE LUBAC, *Cattolicismo. Aspetti sociali del dogma*, Italian tr. (or. Fr., Paris 1938) Jaca Book, Milan 2017, 51. Translated as *Catholicism*, trans. Sheppard, L. & Englund, E, (London: Longman Green, 1950), and later reissued as

a Christian, or an intimate prayer addressed to the Father is always the expression of our sacramental life. An exercise in spiritual life that is not the expression of humanity experienced in sacrament is practically unthinkable. Our activities expressing the life of the Spirit are like the branches that grow from the trunk made up of the sacraments and that reveal our sharing in the divine humanity of Christ.

The redemption of humanity accomplished by Christ is an objective fact that becomes accessible to us in the sacraments of the Church, the body of Christ. But this objective dimension realized by the Father through the Son in the Holy Spirit, this resurrection and transfiguration of humanity into sonship, remains external to human beings until Christ is accepted, until human beings heed this work.

Leo the Great states: '*Quod itaque Redemptoris nostri conspicuum fuit, in sacramenta transivit - that which till then was visible of our Redeemer was changed into a sacramental presence.*'[9] Baptism is the strictly personal replica of universal salvation. With baptism, human beings accept the gift and begin a process of convergence of their whole life, in all its dimensions, to the reception of this gift. This *synergy*, this divine-human correspondence where the energies of God and of human beings in Christ interpenetrate to produce a single action, is the great work of the spiritual life of the Christian. After baptism, spiritual growth will consist of making the life of the Son penetrate all of one's existence

Catholicism: Christ and the Common Destiny of Man, (San Francisco: Ignatius Press, 1988).
    9 *Sermo* 74, *De ascens.* 2 (PL 54, 398).

and in letting it shine through all that we are, until it reaches its full stature. God has given us everything, but we adhere to the gift in a gradual, even though complete way, because we still have to constantly deal with our humanity which remains subject in its more exposed side to the habits and vices of the old man. Our compliance and our efforts to be fully informed by this life are in fact punctuated by time, struggles, by steps ... But what matters is to constantly embrace the gift, constantly turn our gaze to the Giver, and no longer just on ourselves. The Lord never tires of forgiving. In life after baptism, even falls and sin can become opportunities for communion with God, if they mean we are forced to deal with the lack of life within us to make more room for the gift of life that comes from God without our being able to claim anything, neither impeccability, nor individual virtue. It is important to perceive the dependence of our life on the gift received, so that any mentality of conquest, and therefore of failure, no longer returns. This is the work of freely offered compliance. There is no need for an act we have had to undergo, something we had to do, an obligation. In addition, the spiritual practice itself is the expression of this novelty, that is, of the free relationship. Therefore the Christian's maturity is measured by his free adherence. The greater the acceptance, with amazement and emotion, of the Son of God who identifies himself with Adam in his paschal process, the stronger, the freer and more loving will be the Christian's effort to identify with the Christ who died and is risen.

Let us now see how spiritual life grows from the root of our humanity founded on the sacraments, beginning with the sacrament which is the door to this life.[10]

2. *From life destined to die to life that continues*

We have seen that the sacrament in which the Father-Son relationship is extended to include human beings is baptism. Baptism is the sacrament by which the Holy Spirit grafts us onto the Son by giving us divine life. And when the Spirit gives us the life of the Son, he establishes us as his body.[11] Our being rooted in Christ brings us into the communal reality of his body. Precisely because the Spirit of God dwells both in Christ and in each of the believers, God makes all of them a communion in the Spirit, the communion of the children of God all gathered together in Christ as sons in the Son.[12]

Baptism is thus the sacrament in which what we have dealt with in the preceding chapters takes place, namely the passage from a life which leads to death to a life of communion, from a life according to nature to a life according to the Spirit, from isolation to communion, from the individual to the person. This post-baptismal rebirth

10 Cf. Nicolas Cabasilas, *La vita in Cristo,* I, III (*PG* 150, 505AB).

11 Cf. J Corbon, *Liturgia alla sorgente,* (or. Fr. Paris 1980), Qiqajon, Magnano 2003, 173.

12 Cf. JMR Tillard, *Flesh of the Church, Flesh of Christ: At the Source of the Ecclesiology of Communion,* Pueblo Books (March 1, 2001), though taken here from the Italian translation, *Carne della Chiesa, carne di Cristo. Alle sorgenti dell'ecclesiologia di comunione,* (or. Fr., Paris 1992), Qiqajon, Magnano 2006, 16-17.

within the body of Christ is an ecclesial revival because the communal self is discovered to be part of the fabric of the body of communion. This passage is the rite of the sacrament itself. Therefore, as we see in ancient church buildings, the baptistery – shaped like a tomb or a womb – was a separate construction from the church itself, so that after receiving the sacrament, the baptized person then enters the ecclesial community. (figs 7 and 8).

From baptism one passed to the Eucharist, that is to the Church. From the baptistery to the altar. In the Vezelay Basilica we even see how the entire ecclesial space is thought of as the passage from the Baptist to the Messiah, from Baptism to the Eucharist.

At the time of the summer solstice, during which the feast of the birth of John the Baptist is celebrated, the midday sun's rays move along the floor, along the centre of the passage which leads from baptistery to altar (fig. 9).

And in the winter solstice, in the midst of which the birth of the Lord is celebrated, at noon the sun falls on the capitals of the columns lining this passage, carved with images of creation and other Old Testament images, to show that they become legible only in the light of Christ, in which everything was created and redeemed (fig. 10).

In baptism, therefore, we receive a new life that is light (cf. Jn 1:4), and this light illuminates every human being. The life received therefore also has a new understanding, a new way of thinking, because it has a new way of seeing and knowing. This is how we understand the reading of Chapter 3 of John's Gospel, where Christ explains to Nicodemus that to know we must see, but to see we must be regenerated from above. Vision starts from new life, from regenerated life, and knowing is the light that comes from this very life.

Baptism is a milestone for every Christian throughout their days up to the *eschaton*, precisely because it is the founding experience of everything else – life, mentality, feeling, willingness, the experience that *'even when we were dead through our trespasses, made us alive together with Christ'* (Eph 2:5), the experience of *'those who have been brought from death to life'* (Rom 6:13). Not the life lived before death, but a radically new life is the foundational experience that changes our existence into a liturgical existence where there is a continuous exchange between thanksgiving and the manifestation of God's love in our humanity.

Baptism grafts us onto Christ in such a radical way that the life of Christ is more intimate than the life received by parents according to nature.[13]

In baptism, the human being has taken off the 'garments of skin' (cf. Gen 3:21) and 'donned, in water, the robe of the glory that had been stolen [from Adam and Eve] among the trees [of paradise]',[14] the garment of glory and light that the Lord, going down to the Jordan at his baptism, deposited there for us.[15] In fact, neophytes are clothed in

---

13 NICOLA CABASILAS, *La vita in Cristo*, IV, IV (*PG* 150, 600C).

14 JACOB OF SARUG, ed. Bedjan I, cit., 209, It. tr. in S P BROCK, *La spiritualità nella tradizione siriaca*, It. tr. (or. English, *Spirituality in the Syriac Tradition*, Kottayam 1989) Lipa, Rome 2006, 94.

15 "Christ came to baptism, went down and deposited the robe of glory in the waters of baptism, so it could be there for

a white garment, which sums up all the goods of salvation that the Lord gives us in this event.[16] Since clothing is a sort of extension of the body, we can better understand St Paul when he says: '*As many of you as were baptized into Christ have clothed yourselves with Christ*' (Gal 3:27) and you must '*clothe yourselves with the new self*' (Eph 4:24). Clothing, even as a first manifestation of our bodiliness, reveals a new way of experiencing the body which is an ecclesial one, since we are now part of the body of Christ that is the Church. Therefore spiritual life also sees to the relationship with our body and clothing, like a light that comes from the baptismal sacrament itself, as a place which manifests the person rather than nature.

This new life is marked with anointing, in such a way as to be definitively ascribed to the Lord, belonging to him forever.

If baptism confers the beginning of real existence on a person, the anointing with chrism that follows this re-awakening communicates strength and movement to it.[17] This allows the neophyte to fully realize the baptismal

---

Adam who had lost it': JACOB OF SARUG, ed. Bedjan I, cit., 209, It. tr. in S P BROCK, *La spiritualità nella tradizione siriaca*, (or. English, Kottayam 1989) Lipa, Rome 2006, 93.

16 "Our body has become your clothing, / your Spirit has become our habit": Ephrem the Syrian, (EFREM IL SIRO, *Inni sulla Natività*, 22,39, Italian tr. by I de Francesco in ID., *Inni sulla Natività e sull'Epifania*, Paoline, Milan 2003, 368).

17 "Once spiritually moulded and generated ... there is a need to receive the appropriate energy and movement for this birth: this is precisely what the initiation of the divine *myron [chrism]* achieves in us. It causes us to be active with spiritual energy": NICOLAS CABASILAS, *La vita in Cristo*, III, I (*PG* 150, 569A).

energies. The anointing with chrism is therefore the refinement by the Spirit of the image of Christ really alive and active in those who are baptized. The anointing places them under the protection of the saving love of the Son, and their belonging to the body of Christ is so complete that the enemy of human salvation can no longer take possession of them. This is why many of the Fathers describe it in images of strength, because it arms us as soldiers or athletes of Christ.[18] The image that appealed to the ancients was precisely that of the wrestler's anointed body, which prevents the enemy from holding his grip, because his fingers slide off. The First Letter of John states: '*Those who have been born of God do not sin, because God's seed abides in them*' (1 Jn 3:9). Baptism not only brings to birth the new human being, but the anointing unites this being to the One who has conquered death and sin in such a complete way that human beings actively share in the victory over life marked by death.

Marked by the seal of the Spirit – according to the formula of anointing – a symbol of his ownership and his very person,[19] the faithful are organically inserted into one body because the same Spirit who anointed Christ penetrates them completely, placing them within the body

---

18   Cf. PSEUDO.-DIONYSIUS, *Ecclesiastica Hierarchia*, II, III,4 (PG 3, 401D).

19   Chrism is "that unction in which the invisible unction himself, that is, the Holy Spirit, is present in person": AUGUSTINE, *Commentary on the first letter to John, 3,12*, in *Opere di sant'Agostino* 24, Città Nuova, Rome 1968, 1705. These commentaries are available online in English, e.g. https://www.ecatholic2000.com/fathers/untitled-680.shtml#_Toc390303483

of Christ to share in the mission that this body carries out in history as a mission the Father has entrusted to the Son. The anointing therefore clarifies the meaning of the baptismal vocation. The life of baptized persons will be a response to the gift received and a gradual discovery of themselves in this response to the Father's call.

The anointing with chrism in Confirmation confers the gift of the Holy Spirit who is the Lord of communion, the One who pours into our hearts the love of God the Father in such a total and generous way that baptized individuals perceive that they have passed from death to life because they love one another (cf. 1 Jn 3:14). Anointing is the perfection of the gift for which the impetus is given by the Giver in person, who joins with our spirit in a life where two wills by now produce a single fruit of the Spirit (cf. Rom 8:16). The Spirit enables all humanity to freely share and believe in the Lord of love, the Lord who makes his humanity live according to the gift. Therefore this same humanity becomes theophanic. Chrism makes it possible for humanity to be integrally transparent to the life received. Then love, service of one another, openness to the other, acts of mercy toward others are not simply a testimony that the baptized gives of the Saviour, but they become the manifestation of the new life itself that confirms this passage from death to life. In fact, only a life consisting of charity, inclusion of the other, convinces the person of the gift he or she has received.

The chrism, which releases the activity of these renewed human beings, sees that the baptized live their vocation as a sharing in the communion of the body of Christ. Their vocation is communion, and whatever they do in fulfilment of their participation in the body of Christ will be not the search for what is theirs but the affirmation of their belonging to this body. If previously they thought they were realizing themselves by affirming themselves as individuals, endeavouring to stand out so their work would be more visible, now, by passing from death to life, Christians see their fulfilment in being part of communion. Love is not a feeling or an act of the individual, but 'communion of the Spirit' in the one body (see 1 Jn 2:4,8,11,20, etc.).[20] Just as love has a face that is always personal and is irreplaceable, so chrism has Christians understand that their salvation and fulfilment will consist in bringing out communion with others, because what makes them absolutely personal is the way they express communion.

The gift of the Holy Spirit which is conferred, and which brings with it all the richness of his gifts, ensures that everything converges on the unified structure of the body of Christ (cf. 1 Cor 12:13). Christians realize that their life will be fulfilled only by adhering to the body and facilitating the ligaments and sinews (cf. Col 2:19). Their adherence is not only to the head of the body, but is union with others as well, because they begin to experience communion as members of one another (cf. Rom 12:5): the life of one is linked to the life of the other (cf. Gen 44:30).

---

20 Cf. I Zizioulas, *Comunione e alterità,* cit., 339.

3. Food suited to this birth[21]

With baptism and anointing with chrism we are fully entitled to the communion of the body of Christ and begin to live our human nature as persons, that is according to the typical way of God. We begin to live as children, knowing the Father. In a certain sense one could say that, only after our baptismal death and resurrection and anointing with chrism, are we Christians able to begin living the spiritual life, because we find ourselves living with the consciousness of the communal, filial self. It is a consciousness similar to the description in the Gospels of how Christ lived the humanity he had taken on as a child. Spiritual life is possible only when Christians begin to live as children of God, when, therefore, their true ontology is sonship and their true humanity is that of the body of Christ. The life that the baptized have received, together with the gift of the Holy Spirit, makes them live by converging on the body of the Lord. Wherever Christians live the life they have received, this life leads them to converge, to be the Church, the body of Christ. The Eucharist is precisely the sacrament that realizes the Church as the body of Christ and reveals its meaning as the passage to the Father within this body.

In the Eucharist, the ecclesial community gathers 'in one place' (Acts 2:1), in the unity of faith and love.[22] Therefore, in the priesthood of Christ, in the liturgy this

---

21 "The Eucharist fits the birth of those who eat it": THEODORE OF MOPSUESTIA, *Hom, XIV*, 29.

22 Cf. JUSTIN, *Apologia prima*, 67,3; ORIGEN, *On prayer*, 31, 5, etc.

ecclesial community can bring out the body of Christ in the Eucharist as its realization and fulfilment. Christians gathered as the body of Christ, offer what nourishes the life of this world – bread and wine. But, with the coming down of the Spirit, these offerings are converted into the body and blood of the Lord and, by participating in the eternal *anamnēsis*, the eternal memory of total love – that is, the gift of the Son on the cross – they arrive at total gift in Christ. All the humanity that he took upon himself on the cross is made filial, a gift of love. There, everything is accomplished and the Father welcomes him by raising him up. And this Eucharistic Christ who now enters into the eternal memory of the Father through his passage from death to resurrection is constituted by the offering of the faithful gathered as his body. The Church has gathered in a place that belongs to this world and is marked by its history. All who have come together in it are gathered together as the body of Christ, but they have not yet come to the fulfilment of identification with him. They are on their way. But through the offering placed on the altar, by means of the *epiclesis*, they are brought to the *eschaton*, into the kingdom where Christ is already seated at the right hand of the Father.[23] With the Risen One they have passed into the kingdom where neither flesh nor can blood enter, but only the resurrected Son. Therefore the Eucharist is the sacrament of entry into the kingdom. The assembly gathered in one place (*'For as often as you eat*

---

23   S Bulgakov speaks of the Eucharist in this regard as the "sacramental parousia": in *Evvharističeskij dogmat [The Eucharistic dogma],* in *Put'* 20 (1930), 34.

this bread and drink the cup, you proclaim the Lord's death until he comes ...', (1 Cor 11:26) is already a first image of the Church.[24] But a second image is the Church that unites herself to Christ through the bread and wine which are converted by the Holy Spirit into the body and blood of the Lord in the holy liturgy.[25] From now on it is no longer an image, but a substance, because the bread is truly the body of Christ: *'Because there is one bread, we who are many are one body, for we all partake of the one bread'* (1 Cor 10:17). We are no longer a fragile communion still vulnerable to the attack of sin, but with the risen Christ we have entered into the indissoluble unity of the kingdom where there is the realization of communion in its fullest sense. Only in the kingdom, in the *eschaton*, is Christ all in all and there are no other epicentres of glory and power but only one – the Lamb – just as there is only one source of light. The conclusion of the *anaphora* is the exclamation *Through him and with him and in him, O God, almighty Father* ... The Eucharist brings the Church into the full communion of the body of Christ as the realization of filial life before the Father. In fact, it is there that we can pray the prayer of brothers and sisters – the Our Father. And it is in this communion that we 'receive communion'. This food nourishes not only the life of our body for this world, but also our eternal life, the life of the

24 Cf. A SCHMEMANN, *L'eucaristia sacramento del Regno*, (or. Russian, Paris 1984) Qiqajon, Magnano 2005, 9.
25 "When could the holy Church, which is the body of Christ, ask for the consecration with greater reason ... knowing that its Head is born of the Spirit?" FULGENTIUS OF RUSPE, *Libri tres ad Monimum* (*PL* 65, 184-186 and 188).

Son. It is the food that unites us to the Father. Who can unite with the Father more than the Son? We consume the life of the Son to be fully children. The nourishment we consume is also the fulfilment of our vocation.

The communion we enter into through the Eucharist, as we make our entrance to the golden square before the throne of the Lamb, presented by Christ to the Father, is more real than the communion that we can experience among ourselves psychologically and culturally. We are truly what we are only in the Eucharist. Our truth is that of the Eucharist. And when we return from the Eucharist, we are more fully recognized as part of the Son, so much so that 'the Father himself recognizes the members of the Only Begotten',[26] because we become 'blood relatives of Christ more than we are of our parents because we are born of them.'[27]

The Eucharist also means that one of the primary needs of human nature – eating and drinking – as an expression of the individual effort to survive, is founded on Christ who died and rose again and becomes the sacrament of communion. After Adam and Eve's sin, human beings must work and earn their food in order to eat and drink. The Eucharist is the sacrament that makes these human realities of eating and drinking fully realities of Christ, belonging to his way of being. Thus the prayer at the Offertory says: 'through your

---

26 NICOLAS CABASILAS, *La vita in Cristo*, IV, IV (*PG* 150, 600B).
27 NICOLAS CABASILAS, *La vita in Cristo*, IV, VI (*PG* 150, 612CD).

goodness we have received the bread we offer you, fruit of the earth and work of human hands, it will become for us the bread of life.' The Eucharist shows us that humankind will not be saved alone, but together with creation. It is not possible for us to enter the kingdom except through work and with creation. We enter with wheat, with wine, with the things of the earth. The Eucharist has a cosmic and eschatological meaning: it reveals an organic unity between man and creation, but from the perspective of the new creation. Thus, in this sacrament an absolutely unique relationship is revealed between humankind and creation. What sin has darkened, hidden, destroyed, made opaque, returns to being, in this sacrament, something according to God's vision of things, and human beings experience their entire life as a Eucharistic existence where the things that nourish their life, a life that must die, become nourishment for their relationship with God and his communion with creation and other human beings. Spiritual life will consist in extending this sacramental novelty to daily life. One learns to eat, to drink and work from the Eucharist, so that daily life becomes a liturgy after the liturgy: '*I appeal to you therefore, brothers and sisters ... to present your bodies as a living sacrifice, holy and acceptable to God, which is your spiritual worship*' (Rom 12:1). One learns to eat, drink and work by growing from the sacrament. Olivier Clément spoke of 'eucharizing' the universe, recalling that, according to the oldest and best attested tradition, 'the truly radical transformation of man in the Eucharist takes place in martyrdom ... None of us will escape one or other form of martyrdom, in love, in creation, in daily witness, in agony. Then God grants that we become Eucharist.'[28]

4. *Our evil in the body of Christ*

In life according to nature, pain, suffering, death, which we cannot escape, are defeated, along with failure and evil. The spontaneous reaction of an individual self faced with the failure of plans, affirmation, or in the case of an inexorably advancing illness, is normally violent or a sense of total failure, abandonment to a nihilist attitude. In the new life, these situations are also sacramentally founded on the body of Christ. When, for whatever variety of reasons, we succumb to temptation, the bond of love with the Father begins to weaken and we end up focusing on ourselves again, following all the voices that speak of fear for oneself. We find ourselves drowning in waves of evil. Just like St Peter, who had taken his first steps on the waves of the lake but then fear of darkness, the depths, the wind, of the unknown beneath him had shifted his gaze from Christ towards himself and Peter began to sink. The relationship with Christ, which beforehand was strong enough to make even the sea feel solid, now slackens and Peter begins to drown, yielding to fear for himself (cf. Mt 14:22-23). Every sin is a sort of return to the life of the individual, a recovery of the consciousness of the individual self. Every sin wounds love and relationship. This is why it is the return to an isolated existence.

---

28 O Clément, *Maranà tha. Note sull'eucaristia nella tradizione ortodossa*, in *Eucharistia. Enciclopedia dell'Eucaristia*, ed. M. Brouard, (or. Fr., Paris 2002) EDB, Bologna 2004 536 and 539.

The sacrament of reconciliation, then is truly the 'sister of baptism',[29] as the Fathers called it, because it reintegrates us into the body of Christ and gives us back the Holy Spirit as Lord of communion and love. As *Lumen Gentium* (*LG*) states, this sacrament is the sacrament of reconciliation with the Church,[30] because reconciliation with the Father is only possible for children. There is no possibility of becoming children if we are individuals. It is only possible as people who receive the life of the Son, which is already a life of communion. Reconciliation with the Father takes place in the Son. When I am reconciled in his body I find I have even more heartfelt, whole and complete gratitude before the Father. Reconciliation reunites me with the body of Christ, reintegrates me into life as communion and is therefore an increase in gratitude. Reconciliation is the sacrament of gratitude because the Father pulls us out of the mud, washes us, cleans us up, clothes us and makes us guests at his banquet, and all done through no merit of ours. This gratitude becomes a constant dimension. It is characterized by a kind of heartfelt anguish, a sort of prolonged repentance which initially brings tears of pain that turn into tears of grateful emotion. At the beginning, they are tears of sadness, affliction: as children of the Father, from the king's table, we went begging through the muddy streets of the world, squandering the gifts received, not for communion but for ourselves, therefore perverting them and changing

---

29 GREGORY OF NAREK, *Il libro della lamentazione*, 27b, in BL ZEKIYAN, *La spiritualità armena*, Studium, Rome 1999, 279.
30 Cf. *LG*, 11.

their nature as gift. But then the affliction becomes joy, 'joy-grief',[31] turns into the gentle sobbing of someone who realizes the greatness of God's forgiveness and that only by receiving forgivenes does life return to being a gift.

The Church also embeds pain, suffering, illness and death in the body of Christ. The sacrament of anointing of the sick is precisely this – the anointing of the sick person's body, reaffirming that it belongs to the body of the Lord so that the suffering individual, who might be strongly tempted to identify his or her painful condition with suffering nature, with the body and suffering psyche, is reaffirmed and revived in communion with the Son. Anointing is comfort and relief not because pain diminishes, but because relationship is revived and communion is strengthened. Anointing protects the sick so that their filial selves are not overwhelmed by nature due to the trials of pain and the inability to react. It protects them from simply yielding to their fragile and mortal nature.

Anointing reaffirms a person's belonging to a priestly, prophetic, royal people; it re-establishes the bond of love with the body of Christ and, in Christ, with the Father. At the same time it achieves purification, brings forgiveness of sins so that the patient is not defeated by discouragement and does not come to think that he or she is dominated, as a person, by the consequences of sin. Since the wages of sin is death (cf. Rom 6:23), the enemy can prevail when someone

---

31 JOHN CLIMACUS, *La Scala* VII, 11, ed. L D'AYALA VALVA, Qiqajon, Magnano 2005, 195. Available in English online: http://www.prudencetrue.com/images/TheLadderofDivineAscent.pdf

is strongly tested by pain and sickness, things which verge on death, causing them to fall into profound discouragement and severe depression. Pain and sickness instil thoughts of guilt, in themselves or in others. The sacrament thus reaffirms that the person has been saved by the Son of God sent by the Father so that whoever calls on the Lord's name will be saved (cf. Rom 10:13) and whoever believes in him, even if they die, they will live (cf. Jn 11:25). The anointing of the sick is intended to revive the sick person's paschal identity, reminding him or her that baptism has already made them pass through death and that even now, what will die will be the husk of the grain of wheat, while the person is the sprout that appears in the kingdom, in Christ Jesus.

These two sacraments help us grow in spiritual life by giving us a stance based on the *eschaton*, that is, on fulfilment, on the end. These two sacraments tells us that evil will not prevail and that pain, failure, defeat are essential experiences for sharing in the life of the body of Christ. They affirm that sorrow is part of the Church's mission even after Christ's *Pasch*, his Easter, because there is still a becoming that is about suffering endured with love ('*I am now rejoicing in my sufferings for your sake, and in my flesh I am completing what is lacking in Christ's afflictions for the sake of his body, that is, the church*' (Col 1:24). These two sacraments therefore have an essential value for the spiritual life of the Christian, because there is no human life that does not have to face daily failures, discouragement and suffering.

The sacrament tells us that it is not possible to find a sense of failure or pain as such, but that it is only in the relationship of love that we can experience these in a Eucharistic way: we offer up our pain and the Lord gives us the glory of the Risen One. As St Paul puts it: *'I consider that the sufferings of this present time are not worth comparing with the glory about to be revealed to us'* (Rom 8:18). The life of the human being who grows from these two sacraments like a tree growing from its roots, is no longer sensitive to the criteria of this world, its fashions, its values. It is a life that even becomes an open testimony that what is considered successful in the eyes of the world is folly to the spiritual person, and that escape from pain, fragility, failure, illness is simply a lie about the human condition. The spiritual person does not despair that time is passing, the years are advancing, is not concerned about the onset of illnesses. Not out of heroism, but out of the certainty of their outcome, the meaning they find in the wounds of Christ, where these wounds – the offences against him, the slaps, the spitting – were transfigured into the unending light and perfume of the Risen One.

5. *Sharers in the sacrifice of communion*

Two other sacraments – Marriage and Holy Orders – reaffirm humanity's yearning to find fulfilment in union in the body of Christ. Marriage confirms in a sacramental way the traces which have remained in human nature after sin, that help us to glimpse the way of salvation in uniting with another. And the sacrament of Holy Orders bases the human desire to be useful in bringing people closer to God on the divinity and humanity of Christ. It is the desire to serve encounter with the Lord, to be able to make human existence sacred.

These two sacraments are similar in their theological structure. Both of them show that the human being is admitted to sharing in a mystery, one that we cannot know about in life according to nature because it always remains hidden, veiled. We see things in a veiled fashion. The priesthood of various religions, as well as the priesthood of the old covenant, is one of a liturgy which is 'sketch and shadow' (*They offer worship in a sanctuary that is a sketch and shadow of the heavenly one* Heb 8:5), and the union of man and woman according to nature does succeed in overcoming the instincts on which we must rely for such a union. *Erōs* can not overcome *thanatos*. As Jacob of Sarug lets us see so masterfully in his hymn,[32] the meaning of the union of man and woman to form one flesh can only be seen in a vision without a veil. Just as only the bridegroom can lift up the bride's veil, so also the face of the prophecies, anticipations, symbols which are all promises of Christ, is only unveiled when Christ the Bridegroom is revealed. Just as the priesthood of the old covenant was carried out in a temple that was a model of the true sanctuary (cf. Ex 25:40), so also the union of man and woman discloses its meaning only when Paul tells us that what Genesis is speaking about is the union of Christ and the Church (cf. Eph 5:31-32). Christ

---

32 *Omelie 79: Il velo sul volto di Mosé,* Syriac text in Bedjan III, cit., In S P Brock, *La spiritualità nella tradizione siriaca,* Lipa, Rome 2006, 176-195, (or. English, *Spirituality in the Syriac Tradition*, Kottayam 1989).

unites humanity to the Father through his sacrifice, opening the way to the throne of mercy and grace (cf. Heb 4:16) which is found beyond the tent. He is the high priest of the new covenant who carries out his sacrifice once and for all (cf. Heb 9:12). He is the new Pasch and its lamb (cf. 1 Cor 5:7, Jn 1:29,36; 19:36, 1 Pt 1:19; Rev 5 ff, etc.), the new sacrifice and its priest (cf. Eph 5:2, 2:17–3:2; 4:14–10:14); it is he who, by sacrificing his will (cf. Heb 10:9) in obedience to the Father's will, brings humanity through his paschal sacrifice from its present state, belonging to this creation, to the true sanctuary. From Christ's Pasch there is only one priest and one sacrifice. And the ordained ministers of the Church participate in this priesthood and in this priest. The sacrament of Holy Orders thus shows that the ordained minister experiences a fulfilled reality which is Christ. The priestly ministry is to bring about the union of humanity with the Father, in history, through the Church, which is the work of a single priesthood and of the one priest.

The sacrament of marriage touches on something very similar. Husband and wife live by drawing on a reality accomplished by Christ, his priesthood, which united humanity with the Father. As St Paul states, '*this is a great mystery*' (Eph 5:32), the mystery of unity between the Church and Christ, between the body and the Head, between the Bride and the Bridegroom. Husband and wife grow from this reality, from this union. The reality is Christ and the Church, and the two of them are established in this union by the sacrament. Their desire for union is founded on this nuptial love realized by Christ and the Bride – his ecclesial body. In this mystery of the union of humanity with Christ, of the Church with his Lord, realized through the sacrifice he makes to bring about such unity, the two sacraments touch each other. In fact, both find their meaning in the love of people, in a union with God that becomes fruitful in communion. The meaning of priestly service is communion with God and the meaning of marriage is to find fulfilment in the communion of Christ and his body. Marriage according to the spiritual life makes this union grow more and more according to the Holy Spirit, that is according to the union of Christ and his Church, and therefore overcomes the tendency to misunderstand spiritual union as something according to nature. Therefore, the greatest temptation in marriage will be to go back to a life according to nature, according to blood, and to confuse marriage just with family.[33] Marriage, precisely because it is a sacrament, is spiritual. And the family generated by marriage is also called to remain and develop in the order of the Spirit, that is, as Church, because the Church is of the order of the Spirit.

The spiritual life of the ordained minister consists in increasing his ministerial attitude of service. In marriage the primacy of communion is more explicit. The primacy of service is more explicit in the priesthood. Therefore spiritual life sees the ordained minister grow in Christ's priesthood, so that his ministry becomes the place of personal union with the one priest in whose priesthood he

---

33 Cf. A Schemann, *Per la vita del mondo,* Lipa, Rome 2012, 104-114, (or. English *For the Life of the World, Sacraments and Orthodoxy,* New York 1965).

shares. The temptation that the life of the priest is called to overcome is that of misunderstanding his ministry as something pertaining to nature, interpreting it as a function where the person is identified with his role. At this point one slips into religion, and personal union with God is not the first area in which the ministry takes place. It is useless, then, to be making great strides in individual asceticism if the priesthood is mainly understood as a function: it then could become a kind of robe one puts on or takes off. On the contrary, both sacraments have a seal of finality to them, of eternity where communion, and therefore fidelity in relationship, are concerned.

The fact that his ministerial priesthood finds its ecclesial meaning in serving the baptismal priesthood can also be a temptation for the priest. Priestly ministers are at the service of all the baptized so that their priesthood may be the sacrificial life of the Son in them (cf. Heb 13:11-16) and thus may sanctify their daily lives. Even though these two sacraments grow together from the trunk of the body of Christ, contrasts can arise which translate into tensions between the clergy and the laity in daily practice. But if this happens, it is already an indication that we are far from a spiritual life which is the prolongation of the sacramental foundation of union and communion.

From this detailed discussion it can now be seen how our whole spiritual life is founded on this belonging to Christ, on our being grafted onto his body. All our activities, from prayer, to work and, in a more immediate way, charity, are like the branches that grow from this sacramental trunk, which bases our humanity on the humanity of Christ who died and rose again.

All Christians have 'secretly' received the Holy Spirit at their baptism, but for the most part they are unaware of his presence; spiritual life enables one to become aware of this 'secret' sacramental indwelling.

CONCLUSION
THE SYMBOL:
HUMANITY AS REVELATION

If spiritual life begins when we discover relationship in our ontology, then the language with which we express spiritual theology will be a relational language.

We have seen that our life is deeply embedded in the body of Christ which is the Church, with its liturgy and its sacraments. The spiritual life is therefore the development and fruitfulness of this mystery. Precisely because of its grounding and its ecclesial origin it will therefore necessarily be a communal life, will have a relational language, that is, liturgy, where people, with everything they are, continuously manifest all the faces they are in communion with, thus revealing the Face of Christ. Spiritual life, by its very makeup, is a multi-layered reality, because in the gestures, words, feelings of those who live spiritually, one always discovers a deeper presence, a meaning that does not stay just on the surface. Precisely because spiritual existence means living in the other, living in Christ and Christ in us, then nothing is single-layered: everything allows us to glimpse another face, hear another voice, perceive yet another gesture by someone else.

This is why spiritual life, in the way it is made up, expresses itself as a symbolic reality.[1] It lives in the manner of the symbol, that is, as a unity of two worlds, inseparable because united in the person of Christ, in a personal way, a way that is characterized by love freely given. Symbol, when it reveals itself, causes a relational knowledge. In fact, by welcoming it, one enters into communion with the person of Christ who unites the two worlds.

At this point it is necessary to mention a tragic crossroads that has opened up in our history when we abandoned symbolic language and opted for the language of the *summa*.[2] The symbol reveals that what unites the different levels, the different worlds, is a person, Christ, the relationship of love, communion. The dialectic that arose at the end of the Middle Ages shows that the connection between the two worlds and the different levels has become an intellectual operation, a kind of analogy, that is, a resemblance between God and creation that allows one to apply the same term but not mean the same thing. I can speak of God the Creator and human being as creator, but the word I apply to both does not mean the same thing. This means that human beings intellectually understand that there is another level of existence, but they cannot access it because there is nothing

---

1 "All the world's flesh is a symbol of the Spirit": N Berdjaev, *Filosofia dello spirito libero*, (or. Russian Paris 1927-1928) San Paolo, Milan 1997, 149.

2 "*From the Symbol to Summa*; this short sentence is how we have attempted to summarize the evolution of theology and above all of its method between the end of the patristic age and medieval scholasticism": LF Ladaria, *Introduzione alla Antropologia Teologia*, Piemme, Casale Monferrato 1992, 16.

that unites them to that new level. This opens up the tragic path to abstract and illusory knowledge that generates Christian nominalists, or plunges us into the nihilistic dynamics of idealism and moralism.

Instead, symbol emphasizes the participatory aspect and enables things to be always interpreted in Christ, based on Christ, strengthening communion with him.[3] A symbolic, liturgical mentality has its roots in Christ himself because only Christ could say of himself '*Whoever has seen me has seen the Father*' (Jn 14:9). Symbol, therefore, is not a reference to somewhere else, nor the expression of philosophical semiotics, but the relational involvement in a presence. And since relationship is free, symbol is not constrictive, not obligatory. It is revealing and appeals to acceptance.

The spiritual life, precisely because it is the unity of what is human in the Son of God, precisely because it breathes

---

3 "He made all things by His own eternal Word, and gave substantive existence to Creation, and moreover did not leave it to be tossed in a tempest in the course of its own nature, lest it should run the risk of once more dropping out of existence ; but, because He is good He guides and settles the whole Creation by His own Word, Who is Himself also God, that by the governance and providence and ordering action of the Word, Creation may have light, and be enabled to abide always securely. For it partakes of the Word Who derives true existence from the Father ... But all these things, and more, which for their number we cannot mention, the worker of wonders and marvels, the Word of God, giving light and life, moves and orders by His own nod, making the universe one. Nor does He leave out of Himself even the invisible powers; for including these also in the universe inasmuch as he is their maker also, He holds them together and quickens them by His nod and by His providence. And there can be no excuse for disbelieving this" ATHANASIUS, *Against the Heathens*, 41 and 44 (*PG* 25, 84, 88).

the same Spirit of the Son, is necessarily the manifestation of Christ in all that it experiences. This is why it leads human beings to a creative existence where all that is typically human, everything the human being does is experienced in freedom from ourselves, because we are created in the breath of the Spirit, in communal freedom. Therefore the true activity of the Christian is free creativity.[4] Any work Christians do, any talent Christians believe they have is something that the spiritual life urges them to experience in freedom from themselves, not as something which affirms their individual selves, but as somewhere they can manifest free relationships, communion, that is, of the life of Christ. When we are able to do even the simplest work free from ourselves, we do it in a symbolic way. It is then, in that work, that there is a way of existing that reveals the Other of the relationship. And when a job is done like that it really is creative. In fact, from a theological point of view, creativity is what raises the standard of life to a level where life can no longer be attacked by death. And since death means a life locked into the dynamics of human nature and the individual self which is its expression, the desire to save that self, the yearning for self-fulfilment as self-assertion, then we are creative when we do not allow this kind of thinking to infiltrate, because it will pervert life and once again turn it into a dead life.

4 "Creativity is inseparable from freedom. Only someone who is free creates. From need only evolution is born, while creativity is born only of freedom ... Love sweeps away every need and always brings freedom with it. *Love is the content of freedom, love is the freedom of the new Adam, the freedom of the eighth day of creation*": N BERDJAEV, *Il senso della creazione*, cit., 187, 195.

Spiritual life is making room for life in the Spirit, enabling the gift to live in us. And this gift received for ourselves frees our person from attachment to ourselves. When eating, drinking, being together, working, dressing, decorating the house, celebrating, studying, walking, skiing, skating, swimming can allow us to glimpse our freedom from ourselves and enable free relationship to grow, life to grow as communion, then we are contemplating beauty because we feel we are involved in a life free of ourselves, and this creates unity. Contemplation is not just being before a spectacle that spontaneously makes us exclaim how beautiful it is. The spiritual art of contemplation manages to bring out the link between any human situation and Christ. And thus it shows us that salvation is unity. And when we feel united, we perceive beauty. Therefore, we can conclude that the meaning of spiritual life is to become beautiful.[5]

'Blessed is the heart that has crossed the boundaries of every being and is constantly immersed in the enjoyment of divine beauty.'[6]

---

[5] "The personality which is the bearer of the Spirit is doubly beautiful: objectively as an object of contemplation for others; subjectively as a focal point of contemplation which is new and purified of what surrounds it. The saint opens up to us the contemplation of the beautiful, primordial creature and this, our contemplation of the saint, frees us from his corruption: ecclesiality is the beauty of new life in absolute beauty, in the Holy Spirit" P FLORENSKIJ, *La colonna e il fondamento della verità*, (The Column and Foundation of Truth) (or. Russian, Moscow 1914), Rusconi, Milan 1974, 383.

[6] MAXIMUS THE CONFESSOR, *Centurie sulla carità* (*The Four Centuries on Charity*), 1,19 (*PG* 90, 964).

www.ingramcontent.com/pod-product-compliance
Lightning Source LLC
Chambersburg PA
CBHW051946290426
44110CB00015B/2127